CELEBRATING
SUCCESS!™

Fourteen Ways to
Create a Successful Company

RON
FINKLESTEIN

NEW YORK

CELEBRATING SUCCESS!™

ISBN: 1-60037-164-7 (Paperback)
ISBN: 1-60037-037-3 (Hardback)

Published by:

MORGAN · JAMES
THE ENTREPRENEURIAL PUBLISHER™

Morgan James Publishing, LLC
1225 Franklin Ave Ste 325
Garden City, NY 11530-1693
Toll Free 800-485-4943
www.MorganJamesPublishing.com

Cover and Interior Design by:
Tony Laidig
www.thecoverexpert.com
tony@thecoverexpert.com

DEDICATION

This book is dedicated to Spirit, who saw clearly that this was something that wanted to do and would not leave me alone until I did it and to my son Aaron; may the contents of this book help him eliminate the same mistakes I made in starting my business.

TABLE OF CONTENTS

FOREWORD

When I picked up Ron Finklestein's *Celebrating Success! Fourteen Ways to Create a Successful Company* I found myself reading a book that immediately resonated with me. Unlike many business books, this one is chocked full of stories and advice that had such a strong correlation with my business that I read the entire thing in two evenings. It provides a comprehensive description of what successful small companies do to create success. Ron addresses fundamental problems small business owners face as their companies grow and how to overcome them.

The parallels I could draw between the companies in the book and my own were very insightful. When you first start a business, there are certain challenges that need to be met. But it is the late start up and rapid growth periods that are often not covered by books but pose many more challenges.

Fourteen Ways is really a recipe for success with fourteen ingredients that are necessary to be more than a one or two person start up. Is shows you as much about what you are doing right as what you can improve upon.

I strongly encourage business owners and senior managers to read each chapter and reflect on how its message relates to how things happen in your job or business. It provides a process that when adopted, will result in a more successful organization.

Ron McDaniel
CEO
Liquid Learning, Inc.

PREFACE

No one said it was easy to run a business! In fact, few individuals who start companies, or individuals who are stepping up into more demanding roles realize how really difficult it can be. But it doesn't have to be that way!

In this book, Ron Finklestein provides proven ideas and concepts that emerged from interviews he conducted with companies nominated for Celebrating Success! NEO Business Conference!

Each nominated company had a slightly different twist in how they did business but collectively fourteen specific traits or themes emerged.

This book is a recipe on "how to work smarted not harder." I guarantee if you make this book required reading by your executive team and continually hold discussions on how your company can integrate the fourteen characteristics into your company and culture, you will end a more profitable company, one whose staff look forward to coming to work every day and one that provides them a better quality of life and standard of living.

I know because I asked Ron to lead my executive team on lead us through a discussion and implementation of each of the fourteen attributes and work with my team to implement these ideas. We created new business processes that resulted in new products and services. It really works!

Don Philabaum
CEO
Internet Association Corporation

ACKNOWLEDGEMENT

This Greater Akron Business Conference (renamed to *Celebrating Success! Northeast Ohio Business Conference*) and the resulting book would not have been possible if it weren't for the help and dedication of many people. The first person I would like to mention is Don Philabaum, President of IAC. Don had this idea and though it took two years for him to find the right people, he did not let the dream die.

I spent a lot of time trying to find volunteers and it was difficult simply because of the newness of the event. I could not give any assurances about the time commitment. That did not frighten Jo Gilmore, Managing Partner of Group Gilmore. Jo was the project manager for a similar event while in graduate school. Her skill was critical in making this event as successful as it was.

After Jo accepted, it was easier to recruit volunteers. It did not take long for several people to volunteer their efforts. Several committee members handled interviews and information-gathering tasks. Thank you Anita Campbell, Ivana Taylor, Thomas McNamara, Holly Corwon, and Chris Vacca. Holly also doubled as our marketing point person. Tom doubled as sales strategist and Anita did double duty in handling the budget.

After all the interviews were finished, Chris King and Barbara Payne took the interview notes, marketing collateral and nomination forms and wrote the stories that were used by the judges. Those stories are at the back of this book.

Leslie Unger made herself available to coach each presenter if they wanted it.

Pete Effinger orchestrated all the hardware and presentation materials. Alice Hall was responsible for the managing the event-day volunteers. Jean Wales did a super job of managing all the day-of-event activities.

Finally, I want to thank all our sponsors. Without their help and support this event would not be possible: Westfield Bank, Westfield Creative, Greater Akron Chamber, Smart Business, IAC, Kent State, MCPc, American Express, and Air Tran.

Special thanks to Ivana Taylor, John Bothwell and Charles Gilmore for their contribution to this book. In addition, I would like to thank www.2uNews.com for the support I have received in hosting my web site www.yourbusinesscoach.net and the creation of my electronic newsletter.

INTRODUCTION

This book came about as a result of the *Greater Akron Business Conference* (renamed to *Northeast Ohio Business Conference*), held in Akron, Ohio. We did this program because we were tired of hearing bad news. Many of us worked with smaller companies and we knew the negative news we were hearing was not reflective of the successes achieved by these companies.

At the time, a local newspaper was running headlines that looked a lot like: '100,000 Manufacturing Jobs Lost,' as well as stories about Fortune 1000 companies OfficeMax and Roadway being purchased by out-of-state companies. I knew what was being reported by the local media did not reflect the local economy.

In addition, the Information Technology sector throughout the U.S. was in a depression; thousands of jobs were lost. Many people were looking for jobs and realizing there were none, either moved out of the region or started their own companies.

I realized if Ohio was to continue to be a vibrant place where people wanted to live, something needed to be done over and above what the local government was doing. I wanted to get involved and was determined to give something back to the community where I lived for so many years.

The original idea for this event that would become the *Northeast Ohio Business Conference* came from Don Philabaum, President of Internet Association and then-President of *Canal Technology Group*; a group of companies that worked within the community on non-profit activities.

Don approached me working to sponsor an event that focused on small businesses that successfully used technology to grow. I liked the idea and the rest is history.

The *Northeast Ohio Business Conference* was born from a desire to make a difference. The conference would highlight the success of smaller companies encourage conference attendees to purchase services from these companies. From what I could see, there are more than enough resources and there was no reason for any company to spend their money on products and services outside the region.

Don and I were fortunate enough to have some very senior and experienced businesspeople volunteer. I was very surprised by the number of people who wanted to be involved in this activity.

In working through the conference details, it became clear that the future is not in large Fortune 2000 companies. The future is in the thousands of new companies that are being started every day.

To do this we felt it was time to start a change in consciousness by showcasing companies that no one had heard of, but were doing well. These companies were the future of our regional economy. They were doing well and holding their own.

What we did not expect or fully understand was that almost every company had overcome overwhelming odds and moved past some very large obstacles at some point in their existence.

I was amazed by their candor concerning the challenges they faced, the opportunities they identified and the transformation that was required to move forward. For many of these companies and their owners, it was both a personal and organizational transformation.

This understanding revealed several things about leadership. I learned about how important it was to be focused, to believe in yourself and your products. I learned that many of these successful companies did things for their communities and for their customers, because it was the right thing to do. And perhaps most of all, I learned the value of having external advisors and listening to them.

One illustration of "doing the right thing" was demonstrated by ICBS, a local firm providing Internet services. ICBS created a web site, www.holisticonline.com, to help individuals better understand alternative medicines. He did this because his physician wife's patients were asking about therapies they found over the web that were potentially dangerous. She felt they needed a place where they could get reliable information free from subjective input. This web site is totally supported by him, his wife and group of very dedicated individuals who see the value in the service they are providing. This service is free all who choose to use it.

Another company, Software Answers, www.software-answers.com, made a commitment to their clients. The economy was bad and they were running out of cash. Knowing that meeting expectations would cost more than initially expected, they could have backed out of the deal and left their customers hanging. What they did was to continue forward and honor their commitment because it was the right thing to do. Somehow, they found the cash, met their clients' expectations and held on to their core values. Everything worked out for them, taking the high road paid off.

The founders of the Mustard Seed Market & Café, www.mustardseedmarket.com, an organic health food store and restaurant, have a strong belief in service to God. In serving their fellow man, they believed, it allowed them to better serve God. This belief and doing what they love, (providing organic food and qualify vitamins) helped them grow into a robust and successful business.

Each of these companies had a story to tell that went beyond the numbers. My hope in writing this book is to inspire, educate and motivate people who have a business or are looking to start a business. This is not a book about finance, numbers, marketing or entrepreneurship. It is a book of hope, belief, and faith of real companies, real people and real stories.

Hope: because I think our future looks very bright. The number of small companies who are prospering was very exciting and inspirational to me.

Belief: because it takes belief in yourself, your product and service to continue moving forward when things are not going well. The owners of these companies had unshakable belief in what they were doing. They believed they had a valuable product or service to provide.

Faith: because there is so much that can go right, usually from the most unexpected places, to help one realize his dreams. It takes work, but it is so much easier when you know you are not alone: others have been through the same thing and not only survived, but thrived. Many of these organizations are lessons in faith: in themselves, their products and their employees.

It is not possible to talk about all the companies interviewed in detail, and where I received permission, I included the story for your consideration. Each story is unique and has a specific lesson. In most cases, the lessons can be applied to any industry. Enjoy these stories and apply what makes sense to you.

Sincerely,

Ronald Finklestein
President
AKRIS

Celebrating Success! Northeast Ohio Business Conference
(www.neobusinessconference.org)
Co-Founder
ron@yourbusinesscoach.net
330-990-0788

ATTRIBUTES OF A
SUCCESSFUL COMPANY

B y carefully studying companies nominated for awards in the annual *"Celebrating Success! Northeast Ohio Business Conference,"* we were able to pinpoint key attributes that were fundamental to their success. These attributes were then tested with clients to confirm their effectiveness.

These lessons have been broken down into 14 action steps that small companies used to achieve success. Not all companies actively implemented all 14 attributes; some companies utilized only a few attributes while others implemented all of them. These attributes are highly interrelated, and break down loosely into "softer" skills: company culture, customer service, work/life balance, discipline, attitude and risk-taking; and "hard" skills: business strategy, financial & budget, business processes, information technology, marketing, sales and training.

Each attribute could be compressed further but a choice was made to keep them separate. This allowed for a more detailed explanation on topics (such as risk). Depending on the company—

specifically by size—the order and level of influence of each attribute varied widely. We will explore each attribute in detail.

Culture is defined as the "integrated pattern of human knowledge, belief and behavior that depends upon man's capacity for learning and transmitting knowledge to succeeding generations."

Many business owners discussed how hiring the right person was critical and what behaviors they looked for when hiring a new employee. No one specifically used the word culture, but what these employers wanted were people who fit into their corporate culture or who would help shape the culture they were creating.

To simplify, companies wanted to hire employees who expressed a certain attitude or behavior that would make their business more successful, both immediately and long-term. A company's culture was reflected in their attitude on work/life balance, risk taking, customer service and training.

Each company we profiled realizes the importance of **customer service**. However, "customer service" means different things to different people, so let's define it. A customer is defined as "one that purchases a commodity or service." Service is defined as "the occupation or function of one who serves." Together they mean providing service to one who buys your product or service. The concept is simple but the implications and implementations can be quite complex.

Many companies integrate customer service into their culture through training and the design (and frequent redesign) of relevant business processes. In most cases, the business plan dictates how they provide customer service. Once the service level and approach are defined, modifying the business to support the strategy is a relatively easy process.

Discipline is a decisive element for all successful companies. Discipline is also referred to as "focus," "staying the course," or "sticking to their core products and markets." No matter how you describe it or what you call it, it's still discipline. Discipline can be defined as "control gained by enforcing obedience, or order, or to impose order." Maintaining discipline was impossible if the management team did not define a plan and a strategy that the company could follow.

The **attitude** of key managers (the president, owner or business leader) is one of the most important attributes defined. Attitude is defined as "the mental position with regard to a fact or state or a feeling or emotion toward a fact or state." Stated plainly, attitude is the way members of management looks at themselves, their company, their employees, their products (or services) and their customers. Many of the organizations we work with strongly reflect the attitude of the company president. The president knows if and when change is necessary and understands that change "starts at the top."

Because attitude is truly contagious, we discuss it separately, as its own attribute. The attitude of the leader clearly contributes to the corporate culture; all else flows from this culture ... he (or she) sets the tone.

Each of these individuals (and their companies) takes **risks**. Most are calculated risks with clear outcomes in mind. Many business owners bet their livelihood on their company succeeding and most realize they need to change as economic climates change. Each knows it is disastrous *not* to embrace change. Successful business leaders understand that being in business is about managing and responding to change. Companies that succeed embrace change and respond to challenges presented by the market, the competition or changes in general business conditions. Many owners try (and are successful) to create a culture of … *change*. All of the companies that actually made significant changes in their organizations, without exception, wished they had made the change sooner.

The single most critical element identified is the development and implementation of a sound **business strategy or plan**. Though they are not the same, for our purposes, we use the words "strategy" and "plan" interchangeably. We reason that for every strategy, there is an implementation plan and often the implementation is defined within the strategic framework. The strategy could include product development philosophies and approaches, financial goals, and market-orientation with customer-facing strategies. The plan is the implementation of the strategy.

Without exception, it would be very difficult for the companies we help to identify new opportunities and to capitalize on them without a strategy that identifies the basic elements of the business and its overall direction.

An important attribute is the creation of a **financial roadmap and budget** and the discipline to follow it. This plan reminds owners where and how to spend money, and it provides ways to measure progress or shortfalls. Finance is the cornerstone of good business plans. The thought process is: "Why create a plan and not use it?"

Another frequently mentioned attribute of success is the streamlining of **business processes**. We call this *creating predictability*. This is probably the least understood attribute by small business owners. The intention here is to increase productivity and reduce costs while getting the same (or better) outcomes. Business processes are how things are done within a business.

Every company has some processes; some are clearly defined, others are implicit. Each of the companies we interview discusses the need to continuously improve its business processes: to become more efficient and productive, and to respond to market changes faster while providing better service to customers.

Business predictability occurs when a company determines what it does best and creates (and implements, monitors and adjusts) processes that ensure that regular activities occur the same way (measurable and repeatable). When a process is followed correctly, businesses can run without intervention, thus enabling the management team to focus on projects that are more meaningful. These long-range projects may include planning, strategizing and market research.

The next attribute is interesting because we find it within nearly every aspect of operations: the use of **Information Technology**. While technology is important, it is apparent that technology does not have to be complex to be effective. Technology is probably the most important enabler for change that a company can introduce.

Marketing is a nebulous term; it has different meanings for different people. Effective marketing performs different functions around unique selling environments. For example, business-to-consumer enterprises have completely different marketing needs than business-to-business companies.

Generic marketing (or traditional advertising) could help certain businesses to deepen branding and/or top-of-mind-awareness of the company, products and/or services. One-to-one marketing supports high-trust selling. In high-dollar, business-to-business selling environments, marketing automation often supports long-cycle selling. Other companies invest significant time and energy in building a distribution channel. Still others focus on niche markets and attack specific targets with consistency, commitment and diligence.

Every company's approach to **Sales** is different. Some depend on building referral partnerships and strategic alliances, and this is the extent of their sales process. Others aggressively attack the market with direct mail campaigns, cold calls and other forms of direct customer contact. The specific selling approach is usually defined by the marketing plan. Successful owners know that the concept of selling is a process that can be measured and improved, like all business processes. They talk about the importance of having a consistent, measurable and repeatable sales process, and they engage professional sales trainers (with flexibility to customize training to their selling environment) to help create consistency within their selling process.

Training can be defined as "to form by instruction, discipline, or drill and to teach to make fit, qualified, or proficient." Because we live in world of continuous change, it is more important than ever to implement a culture of continuous learning. For many successful owners, continual investment in training is a major attribute identified. Later, we will discuss how training is best leveraged and implemented, and how it supports the business strategy.

Let's move forward and talk in some detail about each of these attributes. In each chapter, we will discuss one specific attribute. At the end of each chapter, you will find questions to test your understanding and to help you incorporate the specific attribute into your business. Your organization may be doing quite well in a specific area and may not know it. In other areas, you may need to make improvements. These questions will help facilitate your understanding of each attribute and the effectiveness of implementing a specific attribute within your organization.

We end with some general comments form the business owners and some direction on how to implement these principles in your business.

CULTURE HELPS ENSURE SUCCESS FROM ONE GENERATION TO THE NEXT!

CREATING A COMPANY CULTURE

In this section, we will discuss the importance of a company culture.

As mentioned earlier, a company culture is defined as the "integrated pattern of human knowledge, belief and behavior that depends upon man's capacity for learning and transmitting knowledge to succeeding generations."

Owners looking to create a culture need to answer one question: "How do I get my employees to express a certain attitude or behavior that will make my business successful, both today and in the future?" This is important because once the correct behaviors have been defined, processes can be created to drive the required behaviors. Once the processes are defined, then systems should be implemented to ensure the behaviors are measured and repeated as required. Areas where attitudes and behaviors are expressed manifest in a company's approach to work/life balance, risk taking, customer service and training. Because of their importance, we will spend time on all of them later in this book.

Healthy companies know how important creating and sustaining culture is for the success of their business. Not all of the companies specifically mentioned the word "culture," but all of them try to create specific behaviors by the programs they implement and the people they hire.

Each of the quotes mentioned below are from successful business owners who know the importance of hiring the right people and the difference it makes in their business. Hiring the right person can be defined as finding someone who has the correct skill set, the right attitude and the ability to fit into the company's culture. These quotes are from companies interviewed for the 2003 Greater Akron Business Conference http://www.akronbusinessconference.org.

"Never underestimate the value and need for hiring and retaining the best employees."

"Build confidence in your clients, your people, your business partners and yourself."

"Surround yourself with good people and employ a team concept."

"Hire as many smart people as you can afford."

"Good personnel hires led to additional good hires; getting the right people 'on the bus' makes all the difference."

"Provide a clear understanding of the company values and define the culture as soon as possible."

"Look for applicants with a good attitude, natural intelligence and a willingness to learn."

"Both the company and employees can benefit when the culture is built on trust and caring."

"Employees learned how far the company and its management team would go to keep good workers. A testimony to the success of a company is the focus on their people; this can be measured by the average tenure of the employees."

A CASE STUDY IN CREATING A COMPANY CULTURE—

Title Company

Gateway Title focuses on creating a specific culture and on hiring employees who are totally in accord with the existing culture. Gateway Title's primary market is homeowners who sell their own homes. After the business was started, significant strategic problems were uncovered. The owner, Rachel (not the owner's real name), had all the business knowledge necessary to start the business: she understood the market, knew the applications and had good relationships with the primary players.

However, Rachel's most significant challenge was that she had underestimated the management skills necessary to run a business. In order to overcome this challenge, she employed a business coach who taught her the value of ongoing education and provided sound management advice in managing the employees. She also made a practice of reading books and listening to tapes on business management and sharing them with her staff.

The first book she read was *Gung Ho*, by Ken Blanchard and Sheldon Bowles. Rachel felt the book was so important that she had her staff meet every morning for 15 minutes to read and discuss it. Response from the staff was so favorable that she now makes attendance and participation in this daily meeting a requirement for all employees.

One of Rachel's favorite tapes is called *A Day in the Zoo*, and it compares different types of people to different animals in a zoo. As we toured the office, Rachel pointed out the different pictures her staff had posted. Each picture reflected a different animal and contained a caption that reflected the primary behavior pattern of the person who reflected that specific animal's behavioral traits. Scenes such as this make it clear that her staff members enjoy the meetings; they contribute and integrate the corporate culture of integrating ongoing learning into their way of life.

An important part of Gateway Title's approach is to set expectations for employee participation. If any employee decides not to participate in the morning meetings, he or she is asked to look elsewhere for employment. Rachel is very clear about detailing expectations during the interview process, so there are never any surprises about ramifications if rules are not followed.

Rachel has created a corporate environment where learning and personal improvement are an integral part of her business practice. This continuous learning led to Gateway Title receiving several awards and being recognized by the state of Ohio as a successful small business enterprise.

A CASE STUDY IN
CREATING A COMPANY CULTURE—
The Doctor's Office

Another organization interviewed was **Allergy and Respiratory Center.**

The cultural difference at this office is clear as soon as you walk in the door. The waiting room does not look or feel like a typical waiting room. Dr. Given' (not his real name) office feels more like stepping into a living room … *his* living room. Every aspect of the waiting area is designed for comfort and safety. The feeling of the office is one of security; you know you are in capable hands.

The doctor spent years creating a theme throughout his practice to make his patients feel safe and comfortable. He believes that if his patients feel safe and comfortable, they would be open about sharing about the activities in their lives that might be contributing to their health problems.

The warm, caring culture shown in the physical environment extends to the personnel as well. Each person we spoke with was open and friendly. Each person who works in his office has the same warm and caring approach. His approach is reflected by each of his employees.

The Allergy Center office was overstaffed compared to other doctors' offices. Each nurse spends (on average) 30 minutes with each patient, capturing all the necessary details. The patients' information is entered into a customized software application that manages all aspects of the office: billing, instructions, medical records and interview notes.

When Dr. Given enters the examination room, he has all the information he needs because it was already captured and entered by one of his staff during the interview process. By reading the notes and asking clarifying questions, he is able to provide better treatment for each patient, which is what he likes best.

One activity the doctor does not like is paperwork. The customized computer system he designed generated all the paperwork electronically, using data captured during the patient's visit—a big relief for the doctor.

The employees liked working there. The average tenure is almost 10 years. Some employees have been with him more than 20 years. Dr. Given does a great job identifying what he wants his practice to "feel" like and he invests heavily to make that dream a reality. All this is working for his patients as well; Dr. Given has less than a 5% cancellation/no-show rate.

HOW DO YOU KNOW IF YOU HAVE PROBLEMS WITH YOUR COMPANY CULTURE?

A culture is defined as the "integrated pattern of human knowledge, belief and behavior that depends upon man's capacity for learning and transmitting knowledge to succeeding generations." Each company has a culture, even if it has not been consciously created. Creating a culture is designed to answer one question: How do I get my employees to express a certain attitude or behavior that is going to make my business successful?

Capturing corporate knowledge is largely a business process. **Please rate your corporate culture on the next page.**

A defined culture goes a long way toward identifying the acceptable behaviors of an organization's employees. In many cases, it allows a company to define the types of behaviors

Company Culture	Strongly Disagree	Disagree	Slightly Disagree	Slightly Agree	Agree	Strongly Agree
Is the corporate culture defined in your business plan?						
Is employee morale high?						
Is employee turnover low?						
Are steps to creating a specific culture defined in your business plan?						
Is employee development part of your corporate culture?						
Have you identified your ideal employee?						
Do you capture your organizational (how you do things) knowledge for future employees to use?						
Do you communicate behavioral expectations to your employees?						

expected from its employees as well as define the type of employee that fits into the company.

It is hard to generalize from a short assessment, but if most of your answers fall into "strongly disagree, disagree, or slightly disagree," most likely you could reduce costs (possibly hiring and training) and improve productivity by defining and implementing a corporate culture consistent with your style.

CAPTURING (COST) A NEW CUSTOMER FAR EXCEEDS KEEPING AN EXISTING CUSTOMER!

CUSTOMER SERVICE

"It's true. U.S. firms, on average, will lose half their customer base over the next five years. And 68% of those customers will leave because of a bad service experience." Mosaix, *Achieving Business Success Through Customer Relationship Management (CRM)*

Much has been written on customer service over the years. From the perspective of a small company, customer service can make or break a company almost overnight.

Mosaix goes on to say that "service leaders (companies which provide superior service to their customers) enjoy the following advantages over their low-service (and often larger) competitors:

- They grow twice as fast.

- They experience a 6% annual market share growth vs. a 1% share loss (they take customers away from their competition).

- They can charge 10% more for their products and still take customers away. Because of this, they enjoy a 12% vs. 1% average return on sales.

The numbers definitely show that the practice of providing superior customer service increases shareholder value and creates a competitive advantage that is worth the investment in customer service tools, techniques and training. Customer Service is especially important when, in many companies, 20% of a company's customers generate 80% of the profits.

> *"Don't be content with doing only your duty. Do more than your duty. It's the horse that finishes a neck ahead that wins the race."*
>
> Andrew Carnegie

If we think about the benefit of building a relationship with a client in human terms, people like to do business with people they like and trust. Not only will a good relationship bring more business from the client, but satisfied clients will be more likely to tell others about the positive treatment they have experienced. Customer satisfaction brings referral business to the organization.

Clients will also tell others about bad experiences. As word spreads about a bad customer service experience (as it will), it can drive others away from doing business with you and your company. Customer service is nothing more than defining and implementing the ground rules on how the company will treat its customers. The customer is looking to understand these rules and wants nothing more than a predictable experience.

Industry statistics show that 68% of customers who walk away from a business relationship do so because of poor customer service. Poor customer service happens at all levels within an organization. In financial terms, a 5% increase in customer retention could result in a 25% to 85% increase in profitability.

Let's look at an example. An associate purchased a cordless phone that had an integrated fax machine. After using the phone for two days, he realized the battery was not charging.

When he called customer service, a company representative told him they would not replace the battery because it was a consumable, and all consumables must be purchased. The replacement battery was more than 30% of the cost of the phone. The attitude of the customer service organization was a problem because this customer expected to purchase a working phone. He was of the opinion that the company should absorb the expense of a new battery.

After repeated calls to the customer service department and asking to be connected with decision-makers higher in the organization, this customer heard the same message, "It is our policy not to replace consumables at no charge." Finally, in frustration, the customer returned the phone and made the decision not buy anything else from this company, including a flat panel TV this ex-customer had been planning to buy. The customer service policy cost the company a total of $2,700. This $2,700 included the cost of the fax machine and the new television. As a small business owner, could you afford to lose $2,700 worth of business?

If your customer service department consistently handles customer problems poorly, how many $2,700 lost opportunities will you have? How many people will this ex-customer tell about his negative experience? How many times do you think this story was told where the company name mentioned? On average, a customer will tell nine other people about an unpleasant experience and only two about a positive experience. How many of your clients are selling against you?

Without exception, the companies that were studied go out of their way to service their customers. These firms understand that it costs almost 10 times more to find a new customer than it does to keep an existing customer.

Moreover, these business owners know that their customers are their windows into the world. Using information from their customers, they are better able to understand how their products are used. This product knowledge allows them to respond faster when a new need is discovered. Successful customer service means that every customer should be comfortable giving you, your company and your product a good reference and a referral.

Each company studied understands the trust their customers place in them when purchasing their products and services. Each does what is necessary to ensure a positive and beneficial experience for their customers. The following comments reflect the overall attitude on customer service:

"Stress the importance of strong customer service; never close a door on a relationship."

"All design and development is done by full-time employees so the customer has many points of contact with all people within the company. All customer questions are answered by the person who is responsible for the issues."

"And always remember, clients don't care about what we think is important!"

"When you stay close to your customer, it is easier to identify a need in the market and focus your efforts on solving meaningful issues for that customer."

Customer Service can make the difference in the level of success a company experiences.

WHAT TO FOCUS ON WHEN CREATING A CUSTOMER SERVICE ORGANIZATION

When creating a customer service organization, you need to ask yourself what kinds of service you are going to provide and how you will provide this service. Is it self-service for a commodity product, personalized service for a complex project, relationship-building with a recurring client base or something in the middle? Correctly answering this question will quickly help you understand what would be most effective in performing your customer-service-related activities.

It is important to know your customer base and the type of service and expectations from this department. This will go a long way toward creating a successful Customer Service department.

SUMMARY

Many customer service attitudes and behaviors are driven by a company's culture. What is your company's attitude toward customer service? Is it a necessary evil or an integral part of customer experience? Is customer service considered an extension of the sales organization and an opportunity to create additional revenue opportunities?

Ask yourself what kind of service you provide your customer.

1. Does this service give you a competitive advantage?

2. Does your product lend itself to self-service? If so, what is the best way to implement this service?

3. How much does it cost you when you lose a customer? Be honest; include sales time, travel expenses, prospecting time, marketing expense, administrative time, lost revenue and the host of other costs that are specific to your business. Now compare this to how much it costs to keep the same customer. Don't forget to add in repeat business that would not be available if you lost a customer.

4. Are you capturing each contact with the customer: sales, support, customer services and management? Does the entire company understand that each employee is a member of the Customer Service department?

DISCIPLINE IS CRITICAL TO ANY SUCCESSFUL ENDEAVOR!

DISCIPLINE

This chapter is about how companies use discipline as an integral part of their business plan. They use discipline in defining the strategy, implementing strategy, managing a budget, creating an attitude and culture, and implementing their strategy.

The discipline derives from their understanding of how the business helps create the life they want. Once they get clear on their expectations from the business, they build a business strategy that describes how the business will support their life's goals. The plan and its execution fall directly from this decision-making process.

Discipline was best described by business owners who said:

"Stick to what you do best and what you are passionate about."

"Focus on just one or two things—that gets everyone focused. Then don't waste time, just take action."

"Test, fail quickly, and move on."

Each company was very focused on driving and measuring the results of their efforts as described in their business plan. They developed their plan and applied the discipline to focus on and work the plan.

Many of the companies had opportunities to engage in activities that were not consistent with their core business. Without exception, they passed on these opportunities, all for the same reason: "It is not our core business and it would distract us from what we are supposed to do."

This ability to choose not to follow an opportunity implied that these leaders maintained the discipline to know their business strengths and core markets while staying focused on those critical aspects of the business. They went through the business strategy and planning process and developed a budget to support the business plan. Then they worked the plan.

If they did not approach their business with discipline, they would lose focus and become distracted from the primary objectives.

If they did not perform the activities as defined in the business plan, it was difficult for them to plan their day, week and month. The business plan answered such questions as:

- How do I know which activities will help me accomplish my goal?

- How do I know I am making progress?

- I have limited resources. How do I best utilize these resources to reach my objectives?

- When do I execute on decision points in my business plan?

Setting aside a regular time for planning was critical. Depending on the individual, they decided which hours of the day were allocated to working *in* the business and which went to working *on* the business.

Of course, they had a huge advantage in running their own business rather than working for someone else. One company's management team did a plan review every Monday at 6:30 a.m.

Each of the business owners walked a fine line between working on the business and working in the business. When they were working in the business, they were selling, shipping products, or dealing with the endless number of problems that face a business owner every day. When they knew what role the business played in their personal lives, they were able to look at this work as an employee would and document the desired outcome. In the very act of documenting, they were working in the business at the same time they were working on the business. When it came time to hire a new employee, they already knew what they wanted this new employee to do, how they wanted that person to do it and how they would track the desired results.

When they worked on business strategy, they looked at the markets, customers and the financial plan, tracking and modifying it as required. They checked their progress against the plan while checking to see if the plan was still valid. This measuring allowed them to keep the pulse of their clients, competitors and markets, while identifying potential new opportunities.

It is extraordinarily difficult to spend time working on the business when the demands of working in the business are so great. It takes discipline to realize and implement a specific time when you work on and modify your company's plan.

The major lesson learned was that these business owners did what needed to be done, not what they wanted to do. They dedicated time to focusing on strategic business issues and delegated less significant tasks to others or moved them to less critical time frames.

These executives and entrepreneurs were very good at determining the action necessary to move forward. They were not afraid to make the hard decisions. It's all very well to set a work schedule and stick to it. It's quite another to spend that time doing what has to be done rather than what you'd rather be doing.

For example, if you spend the first three hours of your peak concentration time reading and responding to e-mail rather than working on those hard challenges that require dedicated thinking time, you're doing the right things at the wrong time. Yes, you do need to read and respond to your e-mail, but in most cases, e-mail is not an intellectually demanding task. Do it when your brain is winding down, not when it's at its sharpest. Do the hard work when your brain is at its best.

Also, consider letting the answering machine or voice mail answer your phone during planning time. It is easy to get so focused to responding to these interruptions that we let them set our priorities for us.

Don't forget to be flexible in responding to unanticipated changes in your schedule. If something comes up that needs your attention, by all means, attend to it. Just make up the time later on. Being disciplined does not mean being rigid.

Don't forget to reward yourself for getting the job done. Nothing motivates people more than to finish a project with the knowledge that when they do, they have full permission to spend time on the other activities that are more consistent with their nature and more rewarding for them to perform.

SUMMARY

Discipline is one of three critical components successful companies are effective at implementing. They understand the plan and create disciplined behaviors that work the plan. They review the plan constantly and change it when necessary. Discipline is knowing when to work on your business and when to work in it.

1. Are you disciplined enough to define your markets, develop a sales and marketing strategy and measure the success of the programs (to create a business plan)?

2. Do you benchmark your organization against your competitors to measure the effectiveness of your strategy?

3. Do you have a schedule that allows you to maximize your time and effort?

ATTITUDE ISN'T EVERYTHING – IT'S THE ONLY THING!

ATTITUDE & WORK/LIFE BALANCE

Attitude is a choice. We create the attitude we need that allows us to move toward our goals. As Napoleon Hill, author of *Think and Grow Rich*, stated:

> "Your mental attitude is something you can control outright and you must use self discipline until you create a positive mental attitude—your mental attitude attracts to you everything that makes you what you are."

Charles Swindoll makes an even stronger statement, and one I am fully in agreement with:

> "The longer I live, the more I realize the impact of attitude on life. Attitude, to me, is more important than the past, than education, than money, than circumstances, than failures, than success, than what other people think or say or do.

It is more important than appearance, giftedness or skill. It will make or break an organization, a school, a home.

> *"The first key to success is deciding exactly what it is you want in life."*
>
> W.L. Hunt

The remarkable thing is we have a choice every day regarding the attitude we will embrace for that day.

We cannot change our past. We cannot change the fact that people will act in a certain way. We cannot change the inevitable.

The only thing we can do is play the string we have. And that is our attitude. I am convinced that life is 10 percent what happens to me and 90 percent how I react to it. And so it is with you."

In the companies that were studied, it was the business owners' attitudes that were upbeat, focused and determined. They all share a desire to learn, and many of them believe in sharing what they learned.

Many companies faced some pretty serious criticism as they created and developed their businesses. As problems surfaced, any of these individuals could have given up and began working for someone else.

As one nominee said, "Don't let criticism get you down," and "Don't listen to the people who say it can't be done."

It is important to have a clear vision and "don't let others talk you out of it." Successful business owners suggest that you follow your dream and "have passion for what you do" and "believe in what you're doing. That makes it fun." Having a good idea was important as well. "Be the best at what you are doing, and don't copy someone's idea."

What became clear to me was that each of these owners had a very clear idea of the role their business would play in their life. It was nothing more than a tool to help live the life they wanted. In being clear in their expectations, they were able to draw significant inner fortitude when necessary because they held to a higher vision. These owners who

> *"Choosing to live your life by your own choice is the greatest freedom you will ever have."*
>
> Shad Helmstetter

were able to hold to this higher focus were better able to handle the emotional challenges that inevitable surfaced.

Many of the companies mentioned "teamwork—the employee bond—is how we made it." The team extended to outside help as well: "Make the leap of faith and trust your advisors."

There were three major areas where business owners excelled. In the first area, they took 100% of the responsibility for what happened in their business, especial when things were not going well. They also mentioned that "as an employer, you have the responsibility for each employee's well being." Secondly, they were quick to give credit where credit was due. They understood they could not do everything themselves, and the employees, coaches, and partners were necessary to their success. Finally, they had the single-minded focus of growing the business, placing nearly everything as a back seat to business growth and development.

Others stressed the importance of taking emotions out of the decision-making process, while emphasizing the importance of "objectivity and independence."

> *"Whatever you focus on is what you get."*
>
> Anthony Robbins

Getting a business off the ground requires persistence and determination. These traits were mentioned several times.

Attitude was also an important element in building a business, especially in customer service. Almost every individual had something to say about customers and customer service: "Customers always have options. So we made sure all of ours were allowed to choose whether to participate in the new functionality or keep it the old way. It was critical to put customer desires first, even if it meant letting them walk away" and "It's okay to charge higher rates and turn down some business."

Almost all of them stressed the importance of goal-setting. It was very hard to know where you are going if you do not have goals. There is a methodology to setting goals to help ensure success and provide focus. Several recommendations for setting goals follow.

1. If you set a goal and it did not work, you need to take a look at why this happened. The importance of goal-setting was stressed repeatedly. If setting a goal did not work for you, do not stop setting goals. Figure out what you did wrong and try again.

2. Goals need to be consistent with our personal values and beliefs. If you create goals that are not consistent with who you are, you will lose interest because

you created an inherent conflict between what you want to accomplish and who you are.

3. When you create a goal, it needs to be your goal, not your wife's or husband's, not your mother's or father's. Yours! It needs to be what you want to accomplish! This is most important for your personal goals. Business goals are usually created for you by clients, markets, customers and supervisors.

4. If you can't get excited about your goals, you will lose interest in them. They will go by the wayside like a fallen leaf or a raindrop, with no more impact in your life. Create goals that you are passionate about, goals that have some inherent risks.

5. Goals must have some inherent risk involved. If there is no risk involved, there cannot be a sense of accomplishment. If you are not stretching yourself and moving outside of your comfort zone, your goals are probably not challenging enough.

6. Many people confuse setting objectives with setting goals. They can have some overlap, but typically goals can be broken down into specific measurable objectives. We may have many goals, but we must decide which ones are the most important and create a plan to satisfy those objectives. Your objectives are the action steps that allow you to move forward. They are not the goal.

7. Sometimes we are so excited about what we want to accomplish that we set too many goals. It is just not possible to focus on more than one or two. Ideally,

focus on one until you have realized that goal. Do not dilute the effort by overextending yourself.

8. Focus on what it looks like to accomplish this goal. Know what it feels like when you have achieved this goal. Plant the end results in your mind and body by seeing and feeling the end results.

9. We need to choose what we will think about. Our thoughts support, or should support, our goals. We cannot have a specific goal in mind if we keep thinking about how it won't work.

10. When you control your thoughts, you are starting the process of controlling your attitude. Decide what attitude you want, and focus on those thoughts.

   "Thoughts lead on to purposes; purposes go forth in action; actions form habits; habits decide character; and character fixes our destiny." —Tryon Edwards

11. Create a plan that will get you where you want to go. Don't overanalyze if you cannot see the road ahead. Just get started, and you will see the proper course of action to take as you move forward. You can update you plan accordingly as things become clearer.

12. Be persistent! Keep a clear picture of your goal in mind, and keep moving forward.

13. Measure your progress. Change your plan, if necessary. A rocket going to the moon is always making adjustments to stay on course. It is always measuring and correcting its flight pattern. Adjust your course, but keep going.

A major attribute of attitude is work/life balance.

"Balance your personal goals and others' expectations."

In our study, it became apparent how focused the business people were and how they pro-tected their time. They had clear goals in mind (business strate-gy), were aware of their time constraints and very selective about where and how they spent their time. Their decisions about time were motivated by how their actions moved them toward their goal.

> "The best way to predict the future is to create it."
>
> Peter Drucker
> *Writer, Teacher and Consultant*

The successful leaders profiled here understand that every person has 1,440 minutes each day, and the way they spend this time directly impacts how much they accomplish and how effec-tive they are.

Amy Merrill of DecisionPoint Marketing made this comment during our interview: "Treat time as a precious commodity, because it is easy to get involved and let the business suffer." This comment clearly reflects the attitude of conference nominees and presenters. This is not to say that these executives do not give of their time. They do. Many are involved in outside charitable activ-ities, and these activities are very important to them.

Another aspect that was interesting was the ways they man-age their time. Repeatedly, calls would be returned after 5 p.m., sometimes as late as 9 p.m. It became clear that anything not directly related to the day-to-day operations of the business, or that was not a marketing or revenue-related opportunity, was one of the last items addressed in the day, implying there is no such thing as an eight-hour workday. We met with some people early in the morning and others late in the evening. Most did a good job of protecting their day.

One individual, Robert (Bob) Dianetti, of RADcom, made a comment that showed a different perspective on work/life balance. Bob loves what he does and his company is very good at doing it. Bob is able to maintain a different perspective than most. His company is an investment of his time, energy and money. He has a very clear expectation of his company to provide the type of lifestyle he wants for himself and his family.

When his company was not performing to his expectations (still profitable but not meeting planned ROI), Bob asked some of the hard questions about his business. He explained to me that as much as he loves what he does, he treats his company as an investment. This investment, if it did not meet certain personal and business objectives, should be treated as any other investment. It was amazing how he was able to be so passionate about his business and yet so completely objective.

At first, his comments were surprising, but as I thought about his statements over the course of several weeks, I realized that this is probably one of the healthiest attitudes I have encountered. His priorities were clear, he was focused on the outcome he expected, he took action that was consistent with both his personal and business values and objectives, and he knew what he wanted. The business was a tool to allow him to create the type of life he wanted.

Many owners and managers are clear about their priorities and focused on the outcomes they want. In most cases, they are clear from a business perspective about the performance they expect, but do not seem to have the personal clarity that Bob has about treating his business as an investment.

Many of these individuals do not differentiate their personal lives from their business lives. Many of the activities they embrace allowed them to marry both their business and personal lives. Many socialized with their clients and claim them as friends

SUMMARY

Owners and mangers of these companies treat their time as their only significant asset they "owned." Decisions on how they use this asset are made based on how the activity supported both business and personal goals. This requires clarity of direction and focuses on decision-making.

What are impressive are their positive attitudes and their belief in themselves and their employees. It was a real thrill to be able to discuss the importance of attitude with these capable individuals. Their beliefs and how they used attitude as a business tool to help them through tough times were both inspirational and motivational.

We must always remember that attitude is a choice. You can determine how you choose to react to a given situation. The conference participants were able to see something positive while in the middle of some very difficult situations.

1. Do you let your situation dictate your attitude? If so, decide how to use your attitude to create the situation you want.

2. The attitude of the company's owner or president helps create the company's culture. How is your attitude

reflected within your company? Has the company created a good-old-boy culture, an autocratic culture, an empowered culture?

3. Does your company set a goal that helps to create the attitude, while supporting the kind of behavior you want from your employees? Remember that systems drive processes, and processes drive behaviors. By defining specific outcomes (behaviors), you can create processes and procedures to measure your success.

4. If you were in charge, what kinds of goals would you set? Would you have a long-term view of the business or quarter to quarter. This attitude will drive the specific decision-making process to focus on the selected outcome.

5. Are you clear about what's important and how you are spending your time?

6. Are you spending your time on activities that move in the direction of your goals?

7. What changes can you make that would allow you to spend more time on what's important to you?

ENTREPRENEURS ARE NOT RISK-TAKERS!

RISK-TAKING

This chapter should be a part of the chapter on attitude. Risk is treated as a separate chapter because of the importance of taking calculated risks and understanding the impact of those risks.

"Some would suggest that entrepreneurs don't take risks. They are so convinced that they have discovered a niche in the marketplace that the idea of failure doesn't occur to them. They are, of course, aware of problems along the way, but they will always endeavor to minimize them." This quote was found on the Internet and was posted by person named Keith. It is used because it fairly summarizes the attitude successful entrepreneurs have about risk.

An entrepreneur is someone who is a reasonable risk-taker, has the self-confidence to take action, is not afraid of hard work and has goals to measure progress; all the while they hold themselves accountable. This statement is not a scientific fact. It is made through observing the companies and talking to the decision-makers.

A reasonable risk-taker is one who defines the opportunity, understands how it solves a problem, and creates and works a plan to address the need. Many of the companies profiled performed their due diligence on the problem or opportunity, understood the risks and had the confidence to move forward.

Self-confidence is an internal knowing. It is a trait that allowed these individuals to move forward when they came to a decision point. Self-confidence usually occurs from having established a track record of success or from an ability to take one's past experience and use that knowledge in new and innovative ways.

The business and financial plan are where the goals are defined and measured. Each of the risk-takers had goals, measured the goals and took corrective action to keep moving forward (see section on Finance & Budget).

Risk implies a lack of certainty in a given situation. There are three primary risks that a company must deal with: technical, financial and social.

1. Technical risk is the degree to which it is difficult for an organization to determine the reliability, capacity and precision of a new technology, or whether newer technology will soon make an innovation obsolete.

2. Financial risk is the degree to which an investment decision (e.g. in personnel, technology or development) will yield an attractive return on investment and whether future returns can be forecasted accurately.

3. Social risk is the degree to which conflict is likely to occur during implementation of an innovation. For instance, will a labor union oppose an innovation because of the labor-saving consequences?

Studies have shown that the most successful people make decisions rapidly. They can do this because they are clear on their values and what they really want for their businesses (and their lives.) The same studies also show that they are slow to change their decisions, if at all. On the other hand, people who fail usually make the decision slowly and change their minds quickly, always bouncing back and forth trying to decide the best course of action.

> *"Test fast, fail fast, adjust fast."*
>
> Tom Peters

Quick decisions can be made and risk reduced when you know exactly what you want your business to look like when it is "done." That is why it is imperative that you clearly define your business's mission and vision and create a forward-looking plan. When you plan effectively, decisions become quick – and risk is reduced because the answer to ANY challenge, when analyzed in respect to your goals, mission and vision – becomes crystal clear. Decisions are typically made quickly, and the actions are implemented.

Many of the companies talked about how difficult it was to make some of the decisions they were faced with. Yet, without hesitation, when asked what they would do differently, each one said they would have made the decision and implemented the change sooner.

Studies have shown that people who take financial risks in the workplace generally tend to be more successful in their jobs, a finding which runs contrary to the idea that risk-taking is simply self-defeating.

This does not presuppose that the necessary precautions were not taken. Precautions are a necessary part of risk analysis. Risk analysis allows for a detailed understanding of the risks associated with the decision. A risk analysis allows for a financial assessment (impact) of each risk. This analysis allows the creation of a forward-looking contingency plan. When things do not work out as expected, the obstacle has already been planned for and an alternative course of action has already been created.

SUMMARY

Facing risk is an inevitable part of life, of making changes, both in our personal and business lives. Know what your strategy is, then accept risks which reward you with progress toward your goals. Good planning and systems can moderate risk. Being a businessperson, it is your responsibility to understand that a big part of what you do is responding to change. With change comes risk. Understanding how to manage risk is significant part of managing success.

WHAT TO FOCUS ON WHEN CREATING RISK-TAKING COMPANY

Being in business is all about taking risks. It is a natural part of daily life. But some changes can carry higher risk than others. The primary objective of introducing a risk-taking culture is not to avoid risk, for that is not possible, but to eliminate as many risks as possible. That is best accomplished by doing a risk analysis, creating contingency plans for possible risks and communicating the change effectively and repeatedly throughout the organization.

END-OF-SECTION ACTIVITIES:

1. What are the consequences of taking a specific risk (costs, market failure, etc.)?

2. What are the consequences of not taking a specific risk (opportunity lost, loss of market position)?

3. What risks do you need to take to get you closer to your goals?

4. What will you do if your risk-taking fails? Do you have a contingency plan in place? Have you completed a risk analysis and assigned dollar values to each risk?

DEFINITENESS OF PURPOSE!

BUSINESS STRATEGY

In this chapter we take a look at an often spoken-of, often misunderstood, and not very often effectively utilized subject—business strategy. To condense a subject that is often in the sole subject of a heavy volume into one chapter, I am limiting our discussion to a number of key points:

- What business strategy is—and what it isn't

- How (well) different businesses approach the execution of a business strategy

- A process for establishing your business strategy

- Making business strategy part of your everyday business activities

The objective of this chapter is to provide an overview of business strategy. As noted above, there is much more detail that can be read on the subject; however, like many business activities, the 80/20 rule applies. That is: 80% of the benefit of having a business strategy can be had from a fairly small (20%)

effort. The real question one must ask is, "Do I need a really well thought out business strategy in order to differentiate my business from that of my competitors?" In today's business environment that may well be the case— and if so, something closer to a 100% effort may well be justified to ensure that your business is a more desirable supplier to your customers than that of your competitors.

Here are some quotes from conference participants.

"Build a strong foundation."

"Change directions when you hit the wall!"

"Startup managers need a working knowledge of financial metrics and reporting, and especially cash flow management. Develop 'business protection' documents early."

"Build on a solid foundation. Take whatever time is needed to do it right. Plan conservatively. Multiple financial supporters are an advantage over a single capital source. 'Partner' decisions are healthier."

"It is important to have a higher vision and purpose."

"Be the best at one thing."

"Don't try to do it alone—get the best advisors. Then listen to them."

It gave him "comfort that he had the expertise to hire the right preferred vendors, plan for contingencies and execute."

"Don't dream or plan within budget constraints. Most great ideas can be implemented within budget AFTER it's been conceived without boundaries."

WHAT BUSINESS STRATEGY IS— AND WHAT IT ISN'T

The term business strategy is one that is widely used, has many meanings to many people and, in general, is not well understood. A good start to thinking about business strategy is to debunk a few common myths:

- *Most business do not have a business strategy:*

  Contrary to popular belief, *all* companies have a business strategy. For companies who have not thought through their mission and how that will be translated into outcomes with value, their strategy boils down to reacting to opportunities and responding to crises as they occur. Such organizations rarely achieve their full potential and often do not survive.

- *A business strategy is something developed and refined every few years:*

  No. Highly successful companies are continuously refining their business strategy to ensure their efforts are focused on the best possible targets. Their business strategy is a living, breathing part of ongoing business activities.

- *Only large companies can afford well-developed, well-documented business strategies:*

Highly successful companies of all sizes have documented their business strategies in such a way that the entire business organization knows the key elements of the strategy, so each employee knows where they fit into the strategy and how the strategy is evolving with the evolving business environment.

- *Formalizing a business strategy can only be done with the assistance of an expensive externally supported effort:*

  Certainly outside support can be used to focus and organize the effort to develop a well thought-out and documented strategy; however, many organizations also have undertaken the effort on their own and have achieved significant success.

- *A properly structured business strategy adheres to and is documented in accordance with the Harvard Business School outline of...:*

  Nope. There are as many formats for successful business strategy development and documentation as there are companies who take the time to formalize the effort.

Okay, so we've agreed that a few of the common myths about business strategies are just that—myths; so what constitutes a business strategy and how does a company go about refining its strategy to ensure maximum company performance?

A business strategy is the company's fundamental concepts of why it is in business. It defines the what, how, where, who of the company's efforts focus in return for customers' business. Clearly, the more detail, focus and general articulation of this strategy that can be contained in a structured document, the better.

The effectiveness of a business strategy comes down to how:

- Crisp the business definition is

- Clearly the key activities needed to execute that business are defined

- Well the definitions and requisite activities are communicated to those who will execute them

The form a business strategy takes depends on the organization—that is, the format for a one-person organization (and one that is going to stay as a one person organization) can be very different from that of a multi-employee organization. For the very small organization it may be just a few notes on paper or a well-understood approach to business on the part of a few key players. For a larger organization, an effective business strategy is probably documented in moderate detail as the management team develops it with broad employee and outside input, crisply communicated to all employees and regularly (and formally) updated to ensure it evolves as the business evolves.

In all cases, the more thoroughly thought out and the more clearly articulated the business strategy, the more successful the execution.

A NOTE ON DOCUMENTATION

While informal documentation is sufficient for many smaller organizations, the process of creating a written record of the company strategies can offer several key benefits:

- It can be a process to clarify thinking, build consensus among key players in the organization and codify agreed-upon results.

- It can validate strategic concepts and the ability to communicate them internally and externally—if you can't write it down clearly, how can you communicate it?

- Once written down, it becomes a useful tool to communicate the strategy clearly and concisely to internal and external stakeholders – employees, suppliers, customers, investors, etc.

- Much like a calendar, a written plan is also a visual reminder of key milestones and tasks.

Writing your strategy down does not, however, mean writing it in stone—this should remain a living, evolving document.

HOW (WELL) DIFFERENT BUSINESSES APPROACH THE EXECUTION OF A BUSINESS STRATEGY

Ultimately, the proof of the pudding is how well the business strategy is executed.

How a business strategy is utilized, like many other activities, is typically found on a continuum—a continuum that runs from the truly excellent at one end of the spectrum to the very poor at the other. As you might expect, the typical company is in the middle of the spectrum and the distribution of companies along the spectrum follows the familiar Gaussian distribution or Bell Curve.

Figure 1 shows the different characteristics of business strategies along a spectrum and characteristics of those business strategies for the different points along the spectrum.

Of course, what level of business strategy excellence is required differs from industry to industry and situation to situation. If your competition does not focus on effective use of a business strategy, then you may not be required to do so either. On the other hand, having an effective business strategy when your competition does not, can be a major competitive advantage.

← 16% →	← 67% →	← 16% →		
Regular poor performer. Organization reacts to opportunity and works to solve problems when they reach crisis stage	**Substandard performer.** Plan is mostly an annual operating plan. Does not react well to new or unusual situations	**The average, company--** with pretty talented employees. Organization typically develops good plans, but struggles with execution	**One of the best in their field--** most of the time, this organization is. The organization Successfully executes a substantial portion of their plan. Slips into non-strategic operation at times	**The top 16% of all organizations.** The organization thinks, plans and acts strategically at all levels at all times
Strategic thinking for the company in the head of one or two key individuals. Typically not known by most of the employees----and management actions often do not reflect the plan	A few key ideas documented in the annual operating plan. May be accompanied by a marketing plan----and some management actions often do not reflect the plan	Plan developed by senior staff, updated as a preface to the annual budget. Rolled out to all employees in annual meeting----plan consulted from time-to-time. Most of the key components not remembered by employees	Plan has input from a wide group of employees, key elements are well known to employees and management actions, for the most part, reflect the plan	Plan is a product of continuous dialog with those who must effect the plan. The whole organization is behind the plan and feels a part of creating the plan.

Figure 1

The boxes under the Bell Curve are shown in two rows. The first row describes the business strategy performance for organizations in the different areas of the Bell Curve. The second row of boxes describes the approach organizations in those sections of the Bell Curve take to the development of a business strategy. As you look at these different characteristics you can easily think of different business organizations you are familiar with and where you might place them on the curve. Clearly, you should also be thinking about where your organization fits on that curve as well. As noted before, this curve is relative. That is, there are few absolutes about the curve, but rather the curve depicts relative performance that can be expected within and industry/market.

A PROCESS FOR ESTABLISHING YOUR BUSINESS STRATEGY

So, you have noted your position on the Bell Curve and, presuming you are not in the right-hand one-sigma + area, you have decided you would like to improve your relative business strategy position on the curve. How do you go about it?

There are many different processes that can be used to develop a business strategy—most all of them have the same basic elements. The most important aspects of developing a business strategy are to follow some kind of a process and to understand what it is that you expect to achieve from the different steps within the process. Most importantly, it is imperative that the process of developing a business strategy be something that is in the hearts and minds of the management team—and indeed the entire organization—undertaking effort. Walking through the steps without a commitment to the end results is a complete waste of time.

A well-developed business strategy has:

- Powerful tactics,
- A pragmatic path, and
- Alignment of the management team

Successful companies invest significant time in developing a business strategy in order to make their future vision a reality.

However, it is not uncommon for the process that develops a business strategy to unconsciously limit input, minimize visibility of ideas and fail to resolve differences within the management team. These situations prevent development of the best tactics and priorities for the business and create risk that the management team will not be aligned around actions, roles, and responsibilities. **The plan may sit on a shelf**—and that is a waste of everybody's time and effort and can be a significant contributor to a reduction in morale.

Achieving an actionable business strategy and an aligned team requires **participation** that is broad but efficient; **consensus** created by building on the best elements from many perspectives, experiences and capabilities, and **agreement** achieved through debate, dialog and resolution of differences. Incorporating these elements provides tactics and targets representing the best thinking of the business, and agreement around the goals, path, actions, and responsibilities.

For the best business strategy development, each participant provides their independent thinking to each element of the plan. Group discussion, with the benefit of visibility of the multiple individual inputs, usually creates additional alternatives that possess the strength of the entire planning group. Figure 2 illustrates a basic strategic planning framework that can be harmonized with existing frameworks or templates that are in use in your business.

The outputs of such a business strategy development process include:

- A plan summary with key concepts and milestones clearly laid out

- Detailed Action Plans linked to each goal

- Resource scoping plans that allow trade-offs of resources against priorities

- Rigorous documentation of the planning work sessions

The benefits of this process are seen in accelerating achievement since the team has:

- An expanded range of alternatives examined because many perspectives have been efficiently incorporated,

- Better tactics as the extended knowledge of many has been utilized, and

- Alignment around the actions and responsibilities through an iterative, collaborative planning process

Today, modern technology offers us some strong tools for developing solid strategic plans by achieving broad-based participation and building needed consensus, even in highly distributed or complex organizations. One such tool is web-based planning software. This can be combined with the guidance of senior experienced professionals in order to assist your team in effectively establishing a comprehensive plan to achieve your growth objectives. The software-enabled approach efficiently permits contributions across time zones and geography, and enables visibility of multiple inputs in order to allow discussions built on shared knowledge to produce strategies, tactics, tasks, metrics, and targets that are understood by all who will be responsible for implementation. Again, the objective is an approach that produces a plan that will be owned by the organization rather than a prescriptive plan developed by a few key members of management or by outsiders.

THE AVANTT STRATEGIC PLANNING FRAMEWORK

PRE-PLAN ASSESSMENT SURVEY

BUSINESS FOUNDATION
- Business Philosophy
- Values & Principles
- Vision
- Communications Plan

EXTERNAL ASSESSMENT
- Market Segments & Opportunities
- Competitive Analysis
- Trend Analysis

INTERNAL APPRAISAL
- Focus Groups & Employee Survey
- Structure & Function
- Operational Strategy
- Quality Systems
- Intellectual Capital
- Change Management

MISSION
What the organization will achieve at a defined point in the future

CRITICAL SUCCESS FACTORS
- Critical Success Factors
- Preliminary Strategic Goals

MARKETING STRATEGY
- Marketing Mix
- Application

DEPARTMENTAL STRATEGIES
- Objectives
- Operationalizing Plan
- Departmental One-Page-Plan

HUMAN RESOURCES STRATEGY
- HR Admin Practices
- Employee Development
- Succession Strategy

FINANCIAL STRATEGY
- Income Statements
- Capital Requirements
- Budgets
- Key Assumptions

OPERATIONALIZING THE STRATEGY
- Critical Success Factors Consensus
- Finalized and Prioritized Strategic Goals
- Resource Scoping

INFORMATION TECH STRATEGY
- IT Value Assessment
- Business Information Assessment
- Opportunity Assessment

IMPLEMENTATION AND CONTROL
- Implementation
- Reporting
- Measurement & Control

ONE-PAGE-STRATEGIC-PLAN
- Vision, Mission & Core Values
- Critical Success Factors
- Prioritized Goals with Milestones

Figure 2

CELEBRATE SUCCESS! *Fourteen Ways to Create a Successful Company*

Using a software-enabled process is not the only way and, where it is not feasible, the same process can be undertaken using "paper and pencil." When the size of the key management team is small, this is probably the most effective approach. With a larger team, it will probably result in a requirement for more time (especially in group meetings) and more meeting discipline to ensure time is not wasted. A good meeting facilitator (prefer- ably one who is not part of the organizational staff) is an essen- tial element here.

MAKING BUSINESS STRATEGY PART OF YOUR EVERYDAY BUSINESS ACTIVITY

Most companies believe intellectually that some form of a formal business strategy is needed to guide operations and to assure good performance. Yet the majority of these companies will admit that their business strategy has failed to live up to expectations and to deliver promised results.

So what is the problem?

In reality, the problem is two-fold. First, many companies continue to use top-down, financially driven, tactically focused processes designed to run yesterday's organizations. Typically, goals are financial and internally focused, and do not get to the "whys" and "hows." Second, traditional business strategies are developed using the 'analysis and recommendation' model. In this model, the business strategy essentially pops out at the end of a one-time effort–usually developed by an outsider with lim- ited input from key stakeholders. By the time the business strat- egy sees the light of day, so much money and time has been invested, that there is little opportunity for (or willingness to listen to) input by those who have to make it happen. Without this input, those charged with implementing that business strategy do not enjoy a sense of ownership in the plan, and flaws may go un-addressed. Neither approach has the flexibility to adjust to changes in the competitive landscape or in the marketplace.

There is a better way

Key thought shifts needed to move toward business strategy development that yields results include:

- Business strategy development is a process not an event
- Good execution is more important than good strategy
- Understanding and commitment are key to execution
- Executing the business strategy is everyone's everyday job
- Continuous monitoring is an essential element of a good business strategy
- Adjustments to the business strategy must be made at frequent intervals

This discussion leads to an important conclusion:

YOUR BUSINESS STRATEGY MUST BE A PROCESS NOT AN EVENT.

Achieving an actionable plan to implement your business strategy requires participation that is broad but efficient; collaboration created by building on the best elements from many perspectives, experiences and capabilities; and consensus achieved through debate, dialog and resolution of differences. A process that incorporates these elements provides tactics and targets representing the best thinking of the business, and alignment around the goals, path, actions, and responsibilities. An alignment-driven business strategy planning process will be a new concept for some. Yet it can provide a comprehensive, efficient means to adjust varying viewpoints behind a single business strategy toward a common objective. Otherwise, even the best plan cannot be executed effectively.

Emphasize Execution

Even the best business strategy will not deliver results if it is not well executed. However, superb execution of a less-than-ideal business strategy will serve an organization very well. There are two aspects of execution that merit comment—-both have to do with the "people" side of the ledger.

It's not enough just to create new tactics around marketing, sales, production and other key functions. "People" issues must be addressed. Competencies— the capabilities an organization must have to succeed— must be present and in the right positions. Giving an individual job goals, performance metrics, and incentives will not produce desired results if the individual lacks the competencies needed to accomplish their part of the business strategy. Sometimes dramatic changes in the business environment create large gaps between what is needed to do a job and the competencies resident within the individual charged with doing it. It is essential that such gaps be closed—through development, addition or replacement. Failure to close the gap when the job is essential to business strategy execution will sow the seeds for broader failure throughout the organization.

Behaviors are the second "people" factor that impacts an organization's performance. Ask yourself the question: "Do I ever see behaviors in the organization that are counterproductive to where we are taking the company?" If the answer is even close to a "yes" or "maybe," then the good news here is there are short-term actions that can be taken to address the issue. Ignoring it, on the other hand, means wasted time, resources, people and money—costs that few companies can afford in today's environment.

Organizations that incorporate behavioral change opportunities and incentives into their business strategies can realize substantial bottom-line benefits if they effectively define expectations and communicate them throughout the organization. By aligning behaviors with its strategic goals in a continuous improvement process, the company has the opportunity to gain significant sustainable strategic advantage over its competitors.

Develop Understanding and Commitment

An effective business strategy is well understood by the organization that must implement it and the organization is committed to the plan. Understanding and commitment are products of communications—and good communications take the form of a dialogue not a monologue.

Consistent, unambiguous communications up, down and across the organization are the lifeline of day-to-day execution. Studies have shown that one of the main reasons why companies do not successfully execute strategy is the lack of employee strategic awareness. Further, if managers put out different messages to their respective business units as to direction, priorities, and goals, redundancies, inefficiencies and errors will result. All detract from the bottom line.

Internal communications are an opportunity to reinforce key messages to the organization. Repetition of the same message by different people in authority is an effective means to not only ingrain the message into everyone's behavior but to underscore that the entire organization "is on the same page." There is strong evidence that when managers communicate well and employees understand goals, organizations perform well.

Make Executing the Strategy "Job One"

Business strategies that really work are totally infused into the company's day-to-day activity—they are not golden guidance delivered from on high. Ensuring that each and every employee understands how their activities impact the strategic plan goes a long way to ensuring that they will not act in a way that is counterproductive or unsupportive.

Continuous Monitoring is Essential

The dynamic, interconnected world we live in makes it mandatory that progress toward goals be measured frequently and adjustments made to accommodate changing conditions. Key customers may change direction unexpectedly, raw material supplies may be subject to price hikes or supply disruptions, and there is always the impact of world events that ripple through all sectors of the economy.

Keep Your Hand on the Steering Wheel

Your business strategies cannot remain static against such a backdrop. Therefore a key element of strategic plans must be a continual questioning of assumptions and measuring of progress. When gaps develop between what is happening and what was planned, changes must be made.

One of the best ways to prepare for developments outside the mainstream of assumptions is to build contingency plans into the strategy. Of course, even contingency plans need to be reviewed at the time they may be needed to assure continued validity. The point is to know about needed adjustments early and to make corrections in small increments. Waiting until things really get out of whack so that major adjustments are needed will destroy momentum and morale and deteriorate performance.

SUMMARY

The essence of a successful business strategy is two-fold:

- Make your business strategy a part of the business' daily life.

- Develop the team along with the plan. The two cannot really be separated.

Failure to recognize these simple ideas has been the Achilles heel of business strategies for decades. In the final analysis, everyone in the company needs to understand how their job fits into the bigger picture and how that bigger picture plays to their individual interests. The synergies that result can carry a company a long way, even in a competitive environment and tough economy where frequent course corrections may be needed.

Developing an effective business strategy is not difficult—but it does require time and effort. There is no "right" approach—but you must be methodical, and getting some outside help to guide your team through the process can often be very beneficial and can improve your team's efficiency.

Most importantly, study after study has shown that businesses with well thought-out and clearly articulated business strategies that are part of the company's daily activity are regularly much more successful than their counterparts who lack such a business strategy.

QUESTIONS FOR CONSIDERATION:

1. Do you know where you want to go?

2. Do you have a plan for where you are going and how you are going to get there? Do you adjust it regularly to accommodate changes in the business environment?

3. Is your team on board? Do they understand and accept the goals, methods and skills required?

4. Are your skills and activities consistent with your goals?

By Charles M. Gilmore, Principal, Avantt Consulting
cgilmore@avanttconsulting.com, 330-867-9860

FINANCIAL GOALS
ARE CRITICAL!

FINANCIAL AND BUDGET

A budget is a plan—a financial plan—that is written down and quantified. It is the financial aspect of the business plan. One reason for a budget is to provide the firm with financial goals. When your plan is absent, how do you know where you are going? How are you going to get there?

A primary purpose of a budget is to force management to think ahead. When plans are made in advance, more choices are available than when operating in firefighting mode. This provides a framework for better decision-making.

A final benefit of budgeting is that it becomes a tool for communication and provides a corporate framework for standardizing activities and communicating goals. The CEO uses the budget process to show stakeholders (including staff) where he or she wants to take the organization.

The master budget is broken down into operating budget and financial budget. The operating budget provides all the information necessary to prepare a budgeted income statement. The financial budget includes the cash budget and financial projections. Once the budget is created, it is helpful to have a budgeting process. Budgeting is the frequent comparison of actual and budgeted items. This comparison allows an organization to investigate variances and to correct problems when it strays from its budget.

The first step in the budgeting process is the completion of an environmental statement. The environmental statement allows the corporation to understand its position with its suppliers, competitors and customers. This includes changes in customer base, technology changes and industry trends. This analysis allows the company to know where there is room for improvement and how much it needs to improve.

Management then develops a set of general objectives. These objectives are a broad-based look at what the firm hopes to achieve. Is the company in rapid growth, facing pricing pressures or customer erosions, planning expansion or facing competitive pressure?

The next step in the budget process is developing a set of financial assumptions. Assumptions include inflation rate, impact of competitors on product prices and sales activities, potential price increases from suppliers, etc. After a clear understanding of the environment is defined, measurable goals should be established.

At this time, I would like to discuss goal-setting. Financial goals, like all goals, must be achievable, measurable and time bound. Achievable goals assume that they are realistic; "stretch" goals are good, but goals that demand too much can create internal and external problems (see the chapter on Attitude).

Measurable assumes that they are being tracked and measured, allowing for corrective action to be taken when variances are defined. Finally, a good goal is time bound. This means that a specific timeframe is assigned for achieving a goal. The budgeting timeframe is usually yearly.

There are many aspects of goal-setting that are important:

- If you are dissatisfied with your company's performance, you need to make sure goals are identified, communicated and measured.

- Make sure your corporate values allow you to support your goals. Goals need to be consistent with these corporate values. If you create goals that are not consistent with the corporate values (usually identified by a company's culture) you create an inherent conflict between what you want to accomplish and corporate expectations.

- Prioritize your goals and fix your attention on the number of goals. The more goals you focus on, the more difficult your business becomes.

- Make goals measurable.

- Create your plan and implement it.

- Measure your progress and adjust accordingly.

Small business owners we interviewed reinforced these ideas with their comments:

"Spend money the right way."

"Making investments wisely—don't fear spending according to a plan."

"Know and measure the numbers. Measure and consider risk and reward."

"Manage the banks. We found that local community banks were not as supportive of small business as the large, regional banks."

"Don't be under-funded. Stay focused!"

"And last but not least: Manage by the numbers and watch cash flow."

Small business owners talked about the importance of using the numbers to take calculated risks. Through having a good handle on the numbers, they were better able to identify opportunities that were consistent with their financial goals.

These same owners talked about making purchasing decisions that were planned. If new technology is needed, was this purchased planned for in the budget?

As variations to the plan were identified, were these variations due to an unforeseen change in the market, customer base, pricing structure or price increases from the supplier? Did this require an adjustment to the existing plan? If so, what was the impact on the rest of the business?

SUMMARY

The budget and planning processes were very important to conference participants. This financial plan defined the existing financial environment, looked at external factors that could impact the company, allowed the company to developed goals and measured the progress against these goals. The process needs to be flexible enough to make changes based on variances and changes in the financial and business environments.

1. Does your company have a financial budget in place?

2. If so, is it being used to make purchasing decisions?

3. Does the budget support the business' strategic plan?

4. When you create your financial plan, do you take into consideration the behavior of your suppliers, competitors and customers?

5. Are the goals of your financial plan consistent with the company's culture? For example, if company growth has been flat for years, it might not make sense to set an aggressive target goal until you are sure the right people are in place and the marketing and sales organization can support this.

6. It might not make sense to compete on price unless you have driven the costs out of the business that allow you to compete on price.

7. Does your company have the tools to measure budget versus actual performance against plan?

CREATE MEASURABLE, REPEATABLE, PREDICTABLE PROCESS!

BUSINESS PREDICTABILITY

Every company has processes; some are clearly defined, others are implicit. Business processes are the way a business does things. When a process is not clearly defined and documented, every situation is unique and requires management intervention. The goal in introducing predictability in your business is to ensure that each employee has a clear understanding of the outcomes you want your client/customer to experience when dealing with your organization, independent of where in the organization that interaction occurs.

Without exception, each company executive interviewed to develop this book explained the need to continuously improve existing business processes, to become more efficient, effective and productive while reducing costs. What many of them did not say or could not articulate was that business predictability is as much about marketing as anything else. Business predictability in your organization should be designed to give your customers a totally predictable experience. This consistency gives them a comfort factor that your organization will always behave in the same way each and every time an interaction occurs. This consistency makes it safe for your customers because they always know the expected outcome.

Business processes include a wide variety of tasks: processing invoices, servicing customers, shipping products and handling complaints. Anything a business does involves a process in some way, shape, or form. It can be measured, modified, streamlined and redesigned (created). If you take a big-picture approach, your business processes include your management information systems. A company's business processes define the interaction between your organization's employees and the ways employees interact within the larger framework of the company, and how successfully the company interacts with the external environment.

How do you know what processes need improvement? Problems manifest themselves in different ways. Some examples of problems in business processes are noted below. Does the process have:

- Inherent delays?

- Excessive transportation and storage requirements?

- Low ownership and/or accountability?

- High rework requirements?

- Significant paper handling?

- The same problems that keep reappearing?

- High waste?

- Poor feedback system?

- Focus on quantity, not quality?

- Long cycle times/long process times?

Many of the companies studied were very clear on the impact of implementing process improvement in their businesses.

" … putting a process in place that ensures that everyone is treated the same (especially important during growth)"

"Continuous improvement is essential, especially based on customer feedback."

"Constantly analyze and improve your business or production processes."

"The way to succeed is continuous improvement; nothing is sacred."

"When business processes are broken down into well-defined segments, individuals who may not have completed an advanced degree can become excellent employees."

"Put people first—have your hiring, education and termination processes firmly in place."

"One secret is to carefully nurture the sales process with a unique approach: he uses an internal sales staff, but because different qualities are valuable in each of the stages of selling—generate/qualify/close … he actually uses different people for each stage."

The business processes used in many businesses have not been designed. Instead, they have evolved over time. This inconsistency leads to business processes that are not as effective and efficient as they could be. Many times, activities occur that add no value to the outcome.

Many companies understand the value of process improvement from the financial perspective but not the overall implications. Business processes:

- Drive a company's culture
- Define how new employees are trained
- Set expectations on how customers are treated
- Propagate the attitude of the company owners throughout the organization

The need to design a business process can occur for several reasons:

- Mergers or acquisitions
- Inefficiencies, cost control
- Lack of process effectiveness
- Competition and global pressures

One of the biggest opportunities made available when performing process improvement is to drive a specific set of behavioral expectations into an organization. **Systems drive processes; processes drive behavior**. Behavior within the organization needs to be predictable. If you are not getting the desired results (behaviors) from your employees, good processes can address the problem.

You cannot manage outcomes, only behaviors. If you are not getting the results you expect, are you managing the behaviors that drive the desired results? Behavioral changes can be implemented through understanding the behavior you want from your employees, implementing the processes to drive that behavior and measuring the results.

It is important to measure the results; otherwise, how would you know how effective the process has become? Many people assume that once a business process is modified that the work is over. That's partially correct. A good process is not only measurable but time bound as well. As your business changes, it becomes necessary to maintain the progress made by "enhancing" your processes.

If you don't do this, the ineffectiveness that created the need for change is reintroduced into the process.

Be careful not to become too internally focused on your business processes. Many companies see great results in designing or redesigning process and over time, they spend more time working on the activities of process improvement instead of focusing on the expected results of the process.

One company I worked for refused to let a proposal go out the door until it was reviewed by more than 20 people. In this process, people would fly in from all around the country for a monthly configuration review meeting. People were more focused on the meeting than on the result of the meeting. This lack of timely turn-around resulted in the sales organization finding ways to circumvent the process in order to be more responsive to the client. In most cases, the configurations being reviewed were not the same configurations being presented to the client.

If you are thinking about implementing a process improvement project in your company, a good methodology (overview) is especially important. Consider the one described below.

- Planning & Organization—Know what you want the redesign to accomplish. For example, do you want to:

  - Drive out cost

  - Make the company more responsive

  - Implement an empowering employee culture

  - Clearly define roles and responsibilities

- Data Gathering & Recording—What data do you need to gather? How do you gather that information? As a business owner, you must know how the data gathering tools and techniques support the project objectives. Will you:

  - Conduct interviews

  - Conduct employee surveys

  - Document the process

  - Conduct site surveys

- Analyze Data—Take what you learned and create a baseline process. After the baseline is completed, you can better understand the implications of making a change in the process.

- Create a Work Analysis Report—Document what you uncovered and distribute the results to the correct audience for validation and approval.

- Redesign the Process—Redesign the process to drive the expected behaviors, cost saving, productivities, etc. defined in the Planning & Organization phase of the project.

- Analyze Risks—Understand the risks associated with the planned changes. Do a risk analysis and create a contingency plan in the event that certain risks materialize.

- Create an Implementation Plan—Many times when processes are changed, companies use the opportunity to implement new technologies. Process improvement does not necessarily imply technology, but it is a reasonable expectation. When technology is implemented, make sure you know the best way to implement and utilize it effectively.

- Create a Cost/Benefit Analysis—The catch here is that the cost/benefit is listed last. In reality, there should be a review of expected costs and benefits with each phase of the project. This step is nothing more than the formalization of what you have learned in the prior steps.

SUMMARY

In summary, poorly designed or implemented processes are the root cause of many problems.

Most processes have not been designed. Well-designed business processes have a clear definition of roles, responsibilities, expected timeframes and process objectives. Well-defined business processes can lead to improved employee morale, improved productivity and reduced costs, and improve bottom-line performance.

END-OF-SECTION ACTIVITIES:

1. Do any of your processes require rework?

2. Do the same problems keep recurring?

3. Is there high waste?

4. Do your processes have poor feedback systems?

5. Is the process cycle time too long?

6. How long are the process delays? Is this a problem?

7. Who owns the process? Who do you go to if the process is not working?

8. Are the people in the process being held accountable for the quality of their work?

9. Does the process have clearly defined roles and responsibilities?

Well-designed business processes have a clear definition of roles, responsibilities, expected timeframes to completion and process objectives that lead to improved morale, increased productivity, reduced cost and improved performance. **Examples of business processes include accounts payable, product development, order entry, etc.** Please rate your business process(es). Feel free to use another sheet for each process if necessary.

Please specify a business process: _____

If you have a check mark in the "agree" or "strongly agree" categories, it is an indication that further investigation is probably required. There could be a very strong payback for this project.

If your check marks fall into the "strongly disagree" or "disagree" categories, congratulations, you are probably doing quite well.

Business Process Improvement	Not Applicable	Strongly Disagree	Disagree	Agree	Strongly Agree
High rework required (doing things over)					
Same problems keep recurring					
High waste					
Poor feedback systems (don't know where in the process the problem is.)					
Long cycle times (Steps within a process.)					
Long process times (the process itself.)					
Process delays (time spent waiting)					
Low process ownership (Who is the person I call who can get the problem fixed.)					
Low process accountability (Who does what activities within the process.)					
Lack of clear definition of roles & responsibilities (Who do I call, and what types of problems do handle.)					

USE INFORMATION TECHNOLOGY AS A STRATEGIC WEAPON!

INFORMATION TECHNOLOGY

Information technology should be an asset to a business and support the business through a clear definition of the role technology will play in the business. This is defined in the business plan.

Implementing a full technology strategy can have benefits that cascade throughout the organization. For example, a tactical use of technology might be where a company decides to build its own PCs using components purchased from local vendors because it thought it was less expensive to do it this way. When the true cost was analyzed, it became apparent that this was not the case: the component cost was less expensive, but the overall costs were higher. For example, when a machine broke and needed repair, it was taken apart, and the broken component was sent back to the vendor. The time to take the machine apart, the shortened warranties, the cost of keeping extra parts on hand and rebuilding the machine, when included in the total cost, made it clear that it was far less expensive to standardize on one vendor and buy those PCs than to build them.

On a more strategic use of technology, another company decided to purchase a software application. It assumed it could implement it itself less expensively than it could by engaging an experienced consultant. Seven years later, it was still not installed correctly. The company overestimated the skills of its employees, did not plan effectively, did not assign the correct resources to the appropriate activity and under-funded the project.

On the other hand, when a technology strategy is defined and implemented as part of the formal business plan, the risk is significantly reduced. The strategy needs to address:

- Company hardware and software standards
- Definition of roles and responsibilities
- Vendor performance management criteria
- Asset retirement strategy
- Buy versus lease analysis
- How technology supports the business plan

Let's discuss how to create and implement an information technology strategy. The approach to information technology must first be addressed as part of the business plan. It must investigate and clarify the roles technology will play in the business. From an information technology perspective, there are only three kinds of projects:

- Those necessary to stay in business
- Those necessary to stay even with your competition
- Those that give you a strategic advantage

For our discussion, we will focus on the third type of projects, those that give you a strategic or competitive advantage.

But first let's define strategic and competitive advantage. A strategic advantage can be thought of as redefining or changing how the game is played. For example, Amazon changed the rules for bookstores. Books can now be purchased online and shipped to your door very quickly and inexpensively. You can read what others think and track what other books were purchased when a specific book was purchased. For example, at the time of this writing, more books are sold over the Internet than are sold in bookstores. This knowledge certainly changed how bookstores function in order to attract and retain customers. Many of the smaller bookstores went out of business, and the larger book stores implemented coffee shops or cafes and invite entertainers to perform at their stores, all in an effort to attract and retain customers.

Wal-Mart is a great example of creating a competitive advantage through the strategic use of information technology. It was successful in integrating the supply chain and driving costs down. This savings was then passed on to Wal-Mart customers. It competes effectively on price and quality because of its strategic use of information technology.

A competitive advantage raises the bar in a specific market or industry. For example, if a manufacturer creates an innovation that allows a product to be produced for 20% less than the industry average, the rules haven't changed but the bar has been raised to a whole new level. Other definitions of competitive advantage could be higher quality, lower cost, speed to market, or improved customer service.

What kinds of problems are suitable and can be addressed by the effective use of information technology? This is a broad question, and information technology (IT) can be used in many markets, on many kinds of applications and on many different kinds of problems. Some of the more effective solutions would address the following business challenges:

- Foreign / local competition
- Deregulation
- Globalization
- Mergers & acquisitions
- Increasing productivity
- Expense control

The challenges generally fall into the following categories:

- Manufacturing & high-tech firms
- Deregulated companies
- Mergers & acquisitions
- Companies facing financial crisis
- Companies under heavy end user demand
- Highly competitive service industries

Many people mistakenly think that management understands IT and will use it effectively. Nothing could be further from the truth, especially in smaller companies. Management, through the effective use of strategic planning, must define the role IT will play within the organization. They must define critical processes and applications, return on investment hurdles and priorities of business objectives and budget. These include:

- Cost benefit analysis
- What constitutes a hard dollar return on investment
- Are soft dollar benefits acceptable?
- What external/internal agencies/departments will be used for benchmarking?
- Where is the biggest impact to the business?
- How is the priority determined?

Hard dollars can be defined as activities that contribute to expenses being taken out of the business or money coming into the business that directly impacts the bottom line. Soft dollars impact the business but not directly. An example of a hard dollar savings would be the elimination of three people from the process. An example of a soft dollar savings would be to increase productivity of the existing staff so that more work gets done by the same number of people. No additional hiring is required.

HOW TO MEASURE IT VALUE

IT does not typically generate value directly. IT adds value by enabling the productive and effective use of existing business processes. This is accomplished by defining the core processes within a business that impact the most and by providing the business objectives that cost-justify moving the project forward. Depending on the processes, the cost justification would include:

- Reducing cost
- Improving productivity
- Increasing throughput
- Increasing market share
- Improving shareholder equity

Each of the business units has a different expectation on how IT should perform and where in the organization the impact would be felt most. For example, if your stakeholders for a specific application or project include chief executive officer (CEO), chief financial officer (CFO), directors, or business owners, the metrics they use to determine the effectiveness of a project might include:

- Revenue
- Net income
- Cost savings
- Earning per share

If the primary stakeholder were the customer, a different set of metrics would be used to understand the value of a project to the organization. Some metrics would include:

- Customer satisfaction
- Customer retention
- Customer profitability
- Customer service levels

If the value is in a business process that crosses multiple departments, divisions or organizational boundaries, value could be defined as:

- Cycle time reduction
- Productivity increase
- Reduced cost

Value can and should be measured differently within the IT organization. These metrics might include:

- Transactions processed
- Staff required

- Overall cost
- Deadlines met
- Maintenance cost
- Training costs

HOW DO YOU APPRAISE A SITUATION?

If you have an immediate opportunity and want a way to appraise the opportunity within the organization, you can use the following checklist to determine how best to move forward. Use this only as a means to identify potential opportunities.

The first step in the process is to identify the opportunities and/or threats being felt. Once the opportunities/threats are identified, take the following action:

- Prioritize the opportunities/threats based on impact to the business plan, if a plan exists. Otherwise, assess the impact to the business overall.

    - Determine the seriousness of the threat or the impact of the opportunity.

    - Make a decision about the urgency of the threat or the potential of the opportunity.

    - Perform problem analysis to validate seriousness, urgency and impact.

The outcome of this analysis will be a list of the top two or three opportunities/threats on which the organization should focus. Once this is complete, take the following action:

- Determine the root cause of the problem.

- Define metrics for solution.

- Brainstorm solutions.

- Select a potential course of action.

- Perform risk analysis.

- Determine budget.

- Create implementation plan.

- Assign resources.

- Assess skill sets.

- Implement plan.

For every technology intervention, there is a customer using the results of the solution implemented. Customers can be defined as either internal or external, so maintaining a customer focus, not a technology focus, is important.

MOVING FORWARD WITH A PROJECT

For customer-facing applications, such as (Customer Relationship Management (CRM), the focus is always on solving a business problem that relates to the customer. You have decided there is a problem and that you want to solve it. What steps do you take to reduce your risk and increase your opportunity for success? If you follow the steps below, you will be will on your way to effective and productive use of information technology.

- Define a measurable goal or outcome.

- Ensure the project aligns the business objective with the IT objective.

- Make sure you obtain executive support for the project.

- Let the business drive the functionality.
- Minimize (ideally eliminate) customization of the software.
- Use trained, experience consultants.
- Actively involve end users in the solution.
- Invest in training.
- Measure, monitor, track.

10 CRITICAL SUCCESS FACTORS

There are 10 steps any business owner can implement to ensure the project progresses forward in a timely manner. The most critical is to ensure the project supports the business plan. If it is not solving a problem or satisfying an objective described in the business plan, why are you doing it? If the project directly supports the business as described in the plan, take the following steps:

1. Create a vision for the project (impact/expected outcome).

2. Define critical success factor. (How do you know you are done?)

3. Define incentive to support the desired change. (Why is the project important?)

4. Name one decision-maker who owns the results and give that person the authority for the project.

5. Define skill sets needed.

6. Determine if the skill sets will be employees or external resources.

7. Find/train resources. (Don't skip training.)

8. Create an achievable plan (realistic, measurable and achievable.)

9. Perform a risk analysis and create contingency plans.

10. Measure progress. Adjust and be flexible.

MISTAKES TO MAKE TO ENSURE A PROJECT FAILS

As we look at the steps necessary to be successful, we need to spend some time understanding why projects fail. The failure rate of projects can be traced to specific actions. These actions significantly increase the odds of failure:

1. Approve a project that does not support the business or provide business value.

2. Don't tell anyone what you are doing or provide regular status updates.

3. Don't implement a change management procedure.

4. Don't budget correctly. (Translated into vendor-speak, win the business first. Address the budget later).

5. Don't use the right people.

6. Underestimate the amount of time the project will take.

7. Don't do an implementation plan.

8. Don't do due diligence on vendors.

9. Don't write a contracts or statement of work that defines deliverables, outcomes, payment milestones,

change management processes, budget, timeframe, required resources.

10. Don't assign roles and responsibilities.

11. Don't train the users.

CREATE A 90-DAY PLAN

We talked about the importance of IT to the organization and how to identify effective projects. We discussed the importance of following the proper methodologies for eliminating risks and improving the opportunities for success.

Let's take a minute and determine what is needed to move forward to make the necessary threats/opportunities a reality in your business. What do you do first?

- Clearly identify the business priority of all stakeholders.

- Define the value you are looking for.

- Set metrics for measuring the value.

- Start measuring –

  - Before, to establish a baseline.

  - In an ongoing manner, to measure changes.

  - After project completion, to see if metrics were met.

THE ACTUAL PLAN

The action plan is broken down in three separate and distinct phases to allow you to take progressive steps. This planning process will allow you to learn at your own pace and get comfortable with the process.

Month 1 - Audit your processes to identify business inefficiencies.

Month 2 - Define and prioritize your company's requirements.

Month 3- Evaluate and select technology vendors.

MONTH ONE OF THE PLAN

During this first month, focus on identifying the speed bumps in your business.

- Review your demand planning strategy, tools and processes needed to forecast customer demand.

- Evaluate how your company manages and mobilizes working capital, inventory, cash and resources to fulfill customers' sales orders. Assess the effectiveness of your company's procurement and inventory management.

- Determine your ability to make decisions in real time.

- Analyze your business processes. Look for opportunities to automate manual processes to shorten the time it takes to move through the supply chain.

- Understand how technology could be used in a unique and special way in your business.

MONTH TWO OF THE PLAN

Define and prioritize your company's business requirements and determine how they support the business objective documented in your business plan.

- Assess your findings and rank your business inefficiencies based on the costliness to the company.

- Categorize your business requirements in must have, like to have and nice but not necessary.

- Prioritize projects based on return on investment (ROI), cost and potential impact on the business.

- Present finding to stakeholders.

- Develop an accurate and realistic project budget and timetable to completion.

- Research best practices.

MONTH THREE OF THE PLAN

You have done your homework in the business. Now it is time to determine who can help you in a manner most consistent with your expectations:

- Evaluate and select technology vendors.

- Chose vendors based on:
    - Technical expertise
    - Knowledge of your industry
    - Other requirements specific to your business

- Calculate full implementation cost, including:
    - License cost
    - Training cost
    - Customization cost
    - Hardware cost
    - Software cost
    - Maintenance
    - Support cost

- Determine the amount of disruption to the business.
  - Downtime
  - Lost productivity
  - Training
  - Learning curve

Congratulations, you are ready to move forward with confidence because you have a roadmap. Remember, having knowledgeable partners reduces the risk and lowers your stress level. Do your homework, find the right partners and trust their judgment.

SUMMARY

Technology is here to stay. It is a core strength to many companies and is used in every company studied to solve a variety of business problems. Understand that the items described above may not be relevant to all businesses. Depending on your business' size, some of the processes described above may be unnecessary. It is important to treat your IT organization as a partner in the business.

END-OF-SECTION ACTIVITIES:

1. Does your business plan have a technology component?

2. Do you have a trusted technology advisor who can help you sort out what technology can work in your company?

3. Does the information technology installed in your company do what you need it to do? If it doesn't, what needs to be changed?

4. Does your IT employee understand how to apply technology to solve your business problems?

5. Are you happy with your technology vendor's performance and customer service? If not, what would you like to do about it?

6. Do you have and track software licenses for all users? Is the process defined?

7. Have you implemented project management tools and techniques? If not, why not?

8. Does your company have a technology asset management program?

9. Do you know what percentage of revenue you spend on IT purchases as compared to your competition?

INFORMATION TECHNOLOGY ASSESSMENT

Information technology is the application of computer systems, tools, software and project management techniques to solve business problems, drive out costs and increase productivity. Please rate your use of information technology.

Are your IT projects designed to:

_____ Create or maintain a competitive advantage

_____ Maintain your existing market position

_____ Necessary to stay in business

If your answers were "strongly disagree" or "disagree" in any area, then there is room for improvement in how IT supports your organization. If most of your projects are "necessary to stay in business" or "maintain your existing market position," there could be room for improvement via implementing IT as a competitive tool in your industry.

Information Technology	Not Applicable	Strongly Disagree	Disagree	Agree	Strongly Agree
Does information technology do what you need it to do? If you picked agree or strongly agree, you can stop right now!					
Do your IT employees understand how to apply technology to solve your business problems?					
Are IT purchases designed to support your business plan?					
Do you have and can you track software licenses for all users?					
Have you implemented project management tools and techniques?					
Are your projects consistently delivered on time and within budget?					
Are your IT vendors performing to your expectations?					
Do you know what percentage of revenue you spend on IT purchases?					

SALES

Our conference participants were not bashful in expressing the importance and impact of a well-designed sales methodology and approach.

Here is what conference nominees and presenters had to say about sales:

"Referrals are golden."

"Relationships and energy count for everything."

"Imagining—and then creating—win-win situations."

> "*Nothing happens until somebody sells something.*"
>
> Arthur H. "Red" Motley

"Get to the sales fundamentals. Identify what is 'good business,' then pursue it relentlessly."

"Focusing on the fundamentals of the sales process 8 hours a day while doing it with measurable repeatable processes."

I've worked with thousands of salespeople in hundreds of companies over the years. The successful salespeople, entrepreneurs and business owners have the following traits in common. First, they set goals; they have a clear vision of what and where they want to go. Many entrepreneurs have a dream but not detailed plans or a roadmap for their journey.

Goal setting is putting your dreams into a written plan. The plan includes benchmarks with dates for tasks to be completed. Those successful people also do something that's interesting. They develop backup contingency plans. When they hit a road-block, they're ready with plan B. In other words, they anticipate hurdles that are sure to emerge along the way and they have a backup plan or strategy in place to deal with them before they smack right into them.

One of the other keys is to know your limitations and accept them. The successful people I've worked with were not afraid to ask for help and they didn't try to do everything themselves. One of the biggest mistakes you can make is thinking that you can do everything without help. Ask yourself, "is this task worthy of my time", or "could someone else do it quicker and less expensively than I can?" Spend your time on issues that play to your talents and strengths. And remember early on in your development or in your business, sales needs to come first. All too often, I find that salespeople, entrepreneurs and business owners spend a lot of time getting ready and getting a lot of technical stuff out of the way but they don't remember that nothing happens until someone sells something.

I subscribe to the S.M.A.R.T. acronym for goals.

Specific: State goals very specifically.

- i.e. "I want to sell ten units of widgets by November 30th of this year with a margin of thirty percent or more."

Measurable: Your goal statement must contain a method of measuring your progress (years, age, date, time, place).

Achievable: You have to believe that you can achieve your goal. It must have reasonableness to it.

- If you are 60 and set a goal to climb Mt. Everest, it may be unreasonable.

Relevant: Your goal must be your goal, not what someone else desires for you. If it is not your goal, you will have no passion for it.

Time Specific: Your goal must have a definite starting point and a stated completion date.

REFERRAL-BASED MARKETING

Marketing is a logical next step that is closely tied to goal setting. Without clear goals, you cannot develop a viable marketing plan.

Word of mouth, referral marketing or referral-based marketing, as I like to call it, is one of my favorite methods for promoting many businesses. Referral based marketing must be focused to be successful.

Prospects obtained from referrals will allow you to:

1. Focus your efforts. You will be focusing your efforts on prospects that know what you sell, have a need or want for what you sell, and would like to discuss it with you, and they have been referred to you by someone they admire, respect and trust. This takes a

lot of the deception and rejection out of the buyer/seller dance.

2. Build trust quickly. Referrals allow you to build trust quickly because some of the relationship that the referrer had with your referral source transferred to you. The referrer normally will speak very highly of you, your professional expertise, and/or your character. This allows you to build trust quickly and effectively with prospects. We have to remember that people do business with people they like and trust.

3. Get to their needs quickly. One of the important steps of being successful in sales is to get prospects, clients and customers to share their needs with you and to share their personal thoughts and feelings. Referrals allow you to accomplish this much quicker and more effectively because you've come highly recommended, they understand why you're there and they value what you bring to the table. Rather than being seen as just another peddler, you've positioned yourself as a true problem-solver and consultant and they willingly share their true needs and true wants with you.

4. Make a good impression early. Edification seems to be a dying art today. If you teach your referral sources how to edify you; in other words, speak well of your character, who you are as an individual, you will find that the sales process moves along much quicker. Because you have been positioned not only as someone with a product or service that the prospect could use but you've also been positioned

as a kind of person, even if they don't do business with you, they would like to meet.

5. Encourage a customer service orientation within your business. Think of the referrer as the goose that lays the golden egg and the referrals as the golden egg. Because you value the golden eggs, and hopefully the goose that lays them, you will find yourself gravitating to more of a customer service orientation within your company. By not spending thousands of dollars on direct marketing campaigns, or hours cold calling, canvassing and prospecting, you can actually spend time servicing your client or customer base.

If you value the referral source, you want to make sure that any client or customer that you get from a referral source is given 110 percent in terms of quality, service and attention. One of the best ways to kill a goose that lays golden eggs is not to take care of one of those golden eggs. Remember, they have a relationship with the person they referred to you. Your referrer's reputation is at risk if you drop the ball and don't follow through.

6. Reduce your non-productive sales activity. I have taught hundreds and hundreds of salespeople how to cold call and yet, in my opinion, it is the least effective method of obtaining prospects and marketing yourself or your company that there is. Am I suggesting that you never do a seminar, that you never make a cold call, that you never do a free talk to a community group such as Kiwanis, Rotary or the local business Chamber?; no. What I am suggesting is that as you become a referral-driven business you will find the need to do many traditional "sales"

activities greatly diminished. I believe in having many legs on your marketing table, with referrals being one of them. I have just chosen to build my business primarily through referrals. I still do talks and I still do seminars, but in much lower numbers.

7. Increase your enjoyment of the sales and marketing function. You'll be in front of a steady stream of people and companies that want and need what you are selling and want to talk to you about what you have to offer.

   For a moment I would like you to close your eyes and imagine that every week you are going out on two or three sales calls and you're going to be meeting with people that you've been referred to. They know what you do, someone has spoken highly of you and they're really looking forward to talking to you. Imagine that every month you were in front of three to five ideal prospects: they use a lot of your goods and services; they understand the value that a professional such as yourself brings to the marketplace; and they're willing to pay a fair price for that service or product. How much more time would you have, how much more fun would you have professionally and how much more financially rewarding would your sales career or business be?

To make this happen, you need to develop an ideal client profile. This would be a great time to grab a piece of paper and start writing as you go through this section. Write down everything you can think of to describe your ideal client or customer. Include such things as:

1. The dollar amount of sales to this client over the course of a year. If you're just starting out, think of what you want this ideal client to be and let's create it.

2. Products or services that they will use. When you look at your value proposition, in other words, when you look at all the goods and services that your company sells, or the ones that you really like to deliver because of margins, production capability, etc. how many of these goods and services will an ideal client utilize? Normally, ideal clients will utilize more than one of our products or services, unless of course, we only offer one product or service.

3. The typical wants or needs of your ideal client. This may require you to go and visit some of your ideal clients and to quiz them a little bit. Who are the individuals that will be using your product or service? We have economic buyers within a company but we also have end users. Who are the people that your product and service has an impact on within a company (or a household if selling to individuals)?

4. Decision-making. Who makes the decision and what is the decision making process that they go through?

5. Financial, social, demographic description. If a company, describe it in detail: annual sales, years in business, number of employees, industry, market segments they service. Is it a single location or do they have multiple branches and locations? Are the decisions made at the corporate offices or are they made at the branch offices? If an individual, what are their assets? What are their age, occupation, marital status, are they male

or female, net worth, is geography important? These are short lists, and I'm sure you can think of many other items you may wish to include here.

6. Environment. What "conditions" create a sense of urgency to move forward and act and what is the decision making process to act now? This becomes extremely important in helping referral sources recognize who they should refer to you and will become extremely important in knowing what questions to ask during the sales process.

I'm sure you can think of other areas to add to this list as you begin to work through this process. This is a process, it is ongoing and it is ever-changing. Your business will grow and change, and so will your ideal client and customer. And as we have all noticed, we are living in a period of extremely rapid change in business and the markets we serve. We both pick up on trends quickly and position ourselves, or we get left behind. This is a document that I would suggest you revisit at least quarterly to make sure that nothing major has changed in what you would like an ideal client profile to look like.

Once you have defined what an ideal client/customer looks like, you can begin to focus your energy in that direction. Just as important, you can now focus your referral sources so that they are only presenting you with referrals that match your ideal client profile. If you can't articulate a clear concise message or description of what an ideal prospect looks like, sounds like or feels like, how can anyone help you get what you really want? Otherwise, you will have to sort through a lot of cats and dogs and deal with the frustration and rejection of cold calling and other more traditional forms of prospecting. A good resource is www.referraldoctor.com.

SELLING

Ok, you now have clear concise goals and a written plan with completion dates and benchmarks to track your success and keep you moving in the right direction. You have created a referral based marketing plan. The next component is a selling system.

Successful salespeople are not born; they are created through hard work, study and following a proven-successful selling methodology. Most great salespeople have a sales coach or mentor and all have a selling system. Think of selling as a game. It has rules, it has regulations and the top performers in this game of selling all have a sales coach or mentor. It always amazes me why people think selling is so easy, and that all you need to do is be a great talker, jump up and down like a trained seal, and people are going to stand in line to do business with you. Unfortunately, that is the stereotypical salesperson; fortunately that's not what the great ones look like.

Having a selling system that you follow religiously is probably more important than whose system you follow. There are a lot of great systems out there some of which may have been created just for your industry, product or service.

Without a selling system that has formalized and written steps on 'what, when and how' well defined, how do you figure where you are in the selling cycle or process? How do you know where you are in the buyer/seller dance? How do you duplicate success and avoid failure? How can you analyze sales that are in process and determine the logical next step or do a postmortem on what could have been a great deal that got away if you don't have a system to rely upon and to use as a template?

Many times companies will hire me to help their salespeople with a particular need such as close more business. "Just teach my people how to close", is what they say. Upon further investigation, I many times find that their salespeople do an okay job of closing - when they are in front of a qualified prospect. The real problem, many times, is that their salespeople do not know how to qualify or disqualify an opportunity. So they have no choice but to treat every prospect the same.

Because these companies have not taken a systematic approach to sales, in other words, they do not have a clearly defined selling process or system, management is unable to really figure out where the real problem is. Is it a prospecting problem, is it a problem of knowing how to qualify and disqualify which opportunities to focus on, or is it a case of too much or too little of some behaviors? Because they have no system, they probably will never know.

Do you have a process or selling system that you religiously follow? Do you have a system to help you qualify and disqualify prospects and determine who is worthy of your time, effort and knowledge and who is not?

Many companies, because they do not have a selling system, don't know what's working for them and what is not because there is little or no consistency to their sales approach. In an effort to fix this, many times they decide to go the route of sales automation or what is often referred to as CRM. Management is then dismayed when the whole sales automaton or CRM project is a huge failure or the sales team refuses to use it. How do you put in a sales automation system when you do not have a selling system? A question worth contemplating, if you or your company is moving in this direction. Be careful or you might end up with automated chaos.

Great salespeople tend to have certain traits that I've observed over the years:

1. They believe in themselves. The really great ones are internally motivated, they have high self-esteem, they expect to win and they do win. They also have the ability to separate rejection of their product or service and rejection of themselves personally. In other words, they are able to separate who they are as individuals from what they do for a living.

2. They follow a selling system or process and learn how to identify where they are within that process or system. Great salespeople have built consistency and repeatability into how they go to market, how they work with prospects, clients and customers. This is one of the reasons they get consistent, predictable results.

3. They build trust and bond with prospects quickly. They understand the concept that people do business with people they like and trust. They adapt their behavioral style to fit the prospect and the situation. If you do not know what your behavior style is and how prospects and others perceive you, a good investment would be to take a quality behavioral, not personality, assessment. If you e-mail me at john@bothwellgroup.com, I will be happy to suggest a couple of behavioral assessments that are relatively inexpensive but extremely effective. I am of the opinion that prospects should see the salesperson that they need to see, experience the salesperson they need to experience to do business. You can

be you on your own time. On the sales call, you need to be whoever the prospect needs you to be.

4. They are good at asking questions and discovering prospects' needs and wants. Unsuccessful salespeople love to talk a lot, especially about themselves, their products and their services, but they spend very little time asking the prospect probing questions and discovering the wants and needs of the prospect.

5. They tend to be enthusiastic about their product or service. In other words, they are true believers in their product or service and you can tell they have conviction. When I say they are enthusiastic, I don't mean they are jumping up and down, saying how great their product or service is, or that they're overly emotionally involved in the sale. What I'm saying is, they're enthusiastic about the benefits of their product or service and they have conviction that what they have is of value and can help the prospect.

6. They are big-picture thinkers and don't get bogged down in minutia. There is a time to dot the i's and cross the t's in the sales process. Covering too much detail and giving prospects too many options turns the entire sales presentation or process into such a complicated jumble of this's and that's that it is almost impossible for a prospect to make a decision. In other words, they stay big picture and only hone in on those details that are germane to the conversation and that the prospect needs to know to make an intelligent, informed decision.

7. They tend to offer solutions later in the selling process than their less-successful counterparts. The successful

salespeople offer solutions only after they have fully identified the problem and discovered what the prospect wants and needs. As a result, the successful salesperson is offering solutions to problems instead of offering features and benefits, which may or may not meet the needs or wants of the prospect.

8. They find out what the implication or impact of the problem or problems are on the company and the individual or individuals involved in the decision-making process. Remember, in many selling situations, we have economic buyers; they have one set of problems and needs and wants and we have end users that are part of that decision making process that have their own unique needs, wants and desires. Successful salespeople identify these and sell to them.

9. Only after building value for their solutions should they discuss money. And they've learned how to help the prospect build a budget by looking at the implications of the problems that the prospect is experiencing and what the return on investment will be based on the solutions that they are recommending to the prospect. If I hear it once a week, I hear it ten times a week, "but they have no budget." It is not unusual for companies and individuals not to have a line item budget for your goods and services. It is your job to help them discover that they have needs and wants and help them discover how much it is costing them in time and frustration not to have you as part of their business life. This is building value.

This is also the key to competing in the global economy. Potential customers may be able to get something cheaper overseas, but that also means that they may not be dealing with you and me. You need to become part of the value proposition that your clients and customers buy. Study after study has shown that one of the reasons that top salespeople are top salespeople is that their clients, their customers perceive them as individuals bringing value to the transaction.

10. When they present, they have a clear understanding of the prospect's needs, wants and desires, their budget and how the buying decision will be made. If you are not doing this, just know that you will probably be fifty to sixty percent less successful than your better-trained and better-coached competitor.

11. They understand sales is a game, I repeat, "sales is a game." They keep it fun and they know they can't get a hit every time at bat. They also know that they will also miss every ball that they don't swing at. The important thing is they are at bat and they decide which balls they are going to swing at and which balls they are going to let pass. They also know that to be really good at the game, they need to practice, they need to study and they need a batting coach.

12. When they don't hit the ball at a minimum, they get a lessons learned. By lessons learned, I mean that they learn a lesson. Spending a lot of time on a sale or on a project and not getting the business is ok if they've learned a lesson from it. Let's face it: education comes with a price. They do not take the loss personally, they analyze it, see what they could have done differently so the next time they're in this situation they're ready.

In closing, really great salespeople understand the value of having a coach. They utilize a systematic approach to sales, they are big picture thinkers, they are optimists by nature and they're trusting. They are also realists and they understand when to cut their losses and they always have a backup plan. They don't let their victories linger too long nor do they let their defeats linger too long. Great salespeople live in the moment. They are focused on the customer, the prospect that they're with right now. They're not thinking about tomorrow's sales, they're not worrying about the deal that got away; they live in the moment.

There's an old saying that if you chase two monkeys, both will get away. Those of you that like to quail hunt, one of the lessons you learn is if you chase the covey, you'll never get a bird. You pick one bird out of the covey, you follow it and you pull the trigger. Professional sales is going to the bank. It is picking one bird, one prospect, one client out of the covey. It's focusing on that client or customer, pulling the trigger, closing the sale or closing the file. A good resource for salespeople is www.bothwellgroup.com. Log on and sign up for their sales thought of the week and peruse their website which is full of tips and ideas.

SUMMARY

Referral-based marketing offers some clear benefits over traditional, cold-call based sales. Knowing who your referrers are and what your "ideal" client is are keys to successful referral marketing. Sales processes need to be clearly outlined and weaknesses identified. Good salespeople are well trained, well prepared, and able to take risks.

QUESTIONS FOR CONSIDERATION:

1. Do you have clear, measurable, written goals? Are they SMART?

2. Are there referrers you should be using to reach out to prospects? Who are they, and what do you need to do to reach out to them?

3. Do you know who your prospects should be? Can you write down their characteristics and target them?

4. Are you getting consistent, repeatable results from your sales staff?

5. Where is the problem in your sales process? Is it closing, or is it qualifying? Both?

6. What can technology really offer to improve your process?

7. Is your sales staff trained to put the customer first? Do they know how to evaluate their contacts and respond to customer needs and wants?

By John M. Bothwell Ph.D.
The Bothwell Group, Inc.
440-356-8774
jmb@bothwellgroup.com

EVERY COMPANY SHOULD BE A MARKET-DRIVEN COMPANY

MARKETING

Marketing played a critical role in the success of many of the companies that participated in the Greater Akron Business Conference. Here is what conference nominees and presenters had to say about marketing:

"Visit peers to learn from their success and failures."

"Don't be afraid to spend money to make your image more professional."

"Clients value having a complete marketing program and the ability to gauge results."

"Be flexible when evaluating the market and keep the big picture in sight."

"Capitalize on [your] signature strength by understanding [your] "crusade" and the emotions [your] customers go through in using [your] product/system."

"He differentiates himself from the competition by knowing who his customers are and building their trust. And he has cloned his system by taking his Excel crusade and building a story and a system around it."

"The key lies in sound customer-centered marketing strategy and your expertise and passion for what you do."

"And make sure to leverage your product to create additional revenue streams from different applications, different markets."

"Growth came from word of mouth – not advertising."

"And always remember, "Clients don't care about what we think is important!""

"Watch carefully. Look for trends, listen to your customers and respond quickly. Most of all — care."

"Realized that as he built his reputation, he was not only selling the "ahs" but also selling "comfort" to his clients."

"It's as much about painting the visual picture to the client as it is about creating the "wow.""

"Proactive communication with clients ensures that expectations are exceeded."

There are as many definitions for marketing as there are marketers and companies. But when you get right down to it, perhaps the best way to define marketing is by its result: *becoming the obvious choice for your ideal customer.*

There are three primary components to becoming the obvious choice –

1. Your crusade. This is the soul and the personality behind what you do and how you do it. It's what makes your organization unique and distinctly different from any other provider. It's the story behind your business and the reason you're in business. Successful organizations don't underestimate the importance of their crusade because they know that their ideal customers recognize its value. It's this very soul behind the business that attracts their ideal customer and keeps them loyal regardless of price.

2. Their desire. Your ideal customer is constantly scanning; both literally and figuratively. They are always looking for solutions that fit them perfectly. They are educating themselves using the Internet, using their friends and using other providers who come to them with offers. They are running partially on data and partially on "knowing what they want when they see it." Successful marketers know who their ideal customer is and have a structure that makes them recognizable as "The One".

3. The system. This is your product, service and the way your customer experiences doing business with you. Your system begins when you or information about your organization "touches" your customer. That's when their experience begins. Building your marketing system around helping your customer make good decisions or giving your customer the best experience with your product or service makes you hard to replace.

When you look just below the surface of products, pricing, promotions and distribution, marketing is visceral. It is all about understands the emotional nuances that our customers have to go through and endure to fill the gap that exists between what they have, what they want and what everyone out there is clamoring to offer.

Marketing is emotional. It's all about understanding the urgency our customers feel, the pain and frustration they endure and the salve our offering provides in the often cold, heartless, indifferent world of purchasing and consumption.

The academics call this buyer behavior. But it's so much more than that. Buyer behavior is a clinical term. But we all know that whether we're buying cars, casters or ball bearings, purchasing is an emotional process. The higher the investment, the higher the emotional involvement in the purchase is.

Here are a few ways to get at the root emotions that drive your customers' buying behavior. By simply understanding the emotional investment they make in their decision, you will be able to position your product or service in a way that will be most meaningful to them and address what they want most.

EXERCISES:

1. When does your customer start thinking about buying what you sell? What situation are they in? What evidence do they have that they need your product or service?

Answering these questions will help you envision the specific circumstances that your customers are in when they start thinking about your product or service. In fact, if you put yourself in your customers' shoes, you may realize that they may NOT be thinking about your product or service when they should be. All of this is important. Write all of this down with as much visual detail and emotional content that you can. Be your customer. Watch your customer; look at their body language and tone of voice. Where is there frustration, how can your product or service help them.

2. What's important to your prospect when they are buying what you sell? You can start by listing the first things that come to mind i.e. results. But how much emotion is there in just results? *Anyone* can promise results and all of us do. That comes right on the heels of "solutions." Be specific and actually use the words your customer would use.

If you were to think about what is important to you when you're buying a car you might say "I don't want to be sold" or if you were buying a drill you might say "I want the salesperson to be knowledgeable about carpentry." If you were looking at landscapers you might say "Come when you say you'll come. Send me a quote when I ask for one or show up when you say you will." You can see the different positioning possibilities any of these avenues can offer. In addition to that, all you would have to do is focus on one area that holds the highest emotional value to your customer and you will beat your competitors hands down.

3. What information does your customer need to make a decision? The law of pricing pressure is that people buy on price when they don't have anything else to compare. If your price is high, there's a good reason for it. Document those things and educate your customer as to what quantifiable value this has to them in the long run.

If you can simply get close enough to your customer to document what the little voice inside their head is saying about the sheer subject of your product or service, you will not only leapfrog your competition, you will become the master of your marketplace.

And when you think about it, that's the goal of any successful business. Marketing strategy and its supporting systems are nothing more than the processes that make that desire a reality.

We live in a buyer's economy. The advent of technology and high-speed information sharing has made the world a much smaller place and that has made it easy for us to become fairly savvy and smart consumers – especially when it comes to high-involvement, high-dollar purchases. Put simply, that means that the days of selling are over and the days of educating, informing, and choosing are here.

SUMMARY

Marketing is emotional – it is understanding what drives your customers' decisions, and how you can address their needs. Price is the lowest common denominator – if you can educate clients on what you can offer beyond price, you can win over the competition.

Questions for consideration:

1. Do you understand who your customers are and what they need? How are you going to find out?

2. Does your marketing tell your customer how you will address their needs, or does it tell them what a great widget you have?

3. What steps do your customers take when making their purchase decision? Where and how can you get their attention?

By Ivana Taylor, ThirdForce Marketing
330-472-0981
ivana@thirdforce.net

WHY IS TRAINING NECESSARY?

TRAINING

The biggest surprise in this entire research project was the different views discovered about training.

Companies use training to accomplish many different objectives that include:

- Creating a company culture

- Driving cost out of the business

- Defining roles and responsibilities

- Improving productivity

- Allowing employees to make a greater contribution to the organization

According to an international study conducted by Coopers & Lybrands 1996, companies that conduct training gave the following reasons.

- Productivity increases

- Greater workforce flexibility

- Saving on material and capital cost

- More motivated workforce

- Improved quality of final product or service

This same study indicates that training is most valuable when linked to the business strategy, when outcomes are clear and when training needs are supported by good HR practices.

Many companies that support training and are effective at linking training to a specific business strategy implement business processes to reinforce training and create a company culture that advocates training.

This training does not always take place in a traditional classroom setting. It sometimes includes restructuring the business process to utilize an individual's strengths, allowing them to build on existing skills. This allows otherwise marginal employees to fit in and make a valuable contribution. In addition to customizing training to allow a company to capitalize on the strength of the employees, other methods of training are implemented regularly:

- Internet-based training/Computer-based training

- Situational-based training

- Self-paced training

Internet-based training is composed of training that can be taken by the employee at any time that is convenient. As Internet-based training becomes more and more sophisticated, abundant and less expensive, more and more companies will utilize this training tool. Currently, there is a wide range of training available under a wide variety of topics.

Situation-based training is designed to facilitate and conduct realistic, state-of-the-art aviation training exercises for aviation combat units scheduled to deploy to combat situations. Soldiers and civilians are put through a series of situational-based training scenarios using high-tech virtual simulators, advanced communications and integrated operations systems. Other situation-based training programs exist for business coaches, airplane pilots and business executives.

Self-paced training is probably the most popular. People learn at different paces and in different ways. Good self-paced training will recognize this and present the material in ways that give the student the best opportunity to learn. All of the training styles reflect methods to test the comprehension of the student and offer a review of the material, where needed.

The workforce is changing, the markets are changing and the general population has access to more information than ever before. Continued personal and professional development are needed. Each of us must understand that continued improvement of our existing skills and acquisition of new skills are critical.

Companies that understand this environment of continuous learning can contribute to the effectiveness of the organization and impact the bottom line.

SUMMARY

Education, to be the most valuable, must be linked to the business strategy, have clear outcomes and be supported by good HR practices. Changes in the regional (and global) economy will require a more skilled workforce. Training, in the past, was considered a perk. With the fast-changing world, training takes on a critical role. Training can drive personal and business productivity and be used to change the culture of an organization. Training can no longer be used as a reward system. Training must be implemented in any organization. This can lead to a "learning organization" and can lead to new opportunities.

WHAT TO FOCUS ON WHEN CREATING A TRAINING PLAN?

All training needs to address:

- How it supports the objectives in the strategic plan (if applicable)

- What is the return on investment of the training?

- How will it address the growth path for the individual?

- What policies or procedures exist (or will be implemented) to reinforce what was learned?

Sometimes training has nothing to do with the strategic plan. There is a chance to capitalize on an opportunity, and it just makes sense. In this situation, return on investment is very important. It is necessary to clearly understand the reason for, and expected outcome of, the training.

Training that is mandated by the strategic plan is usually dictated by the business situation. This might include training every employee on the new software being installed or implementing a training program mandated by government or agency regulations.

Sound human resource practices that reinforce what was learned and provide a vehicle to allow the employee to use the recently acquired skill are very important.

END-OF-SECTION ACTIVITIES:

1. Does your company have a training plan in place that is structured to support the business strategy?

2. Is training measured to determine the financial and productivity impact to the organization?

3. How do you measure the impact of training in your organization?

4. Are your employees motivated to keep their skills current? If not, why not?

BRINGING IT
ALL TOGETHER -
TAKING CONTROL
OF YOUR DESTINY

You read about all the different possibilities in moving your company forward. It can be confusing. So where do you start?

There are three attributes that are critical to becoming more successful. These are the three considered to be the most important. The first is attitude, the second is business strategy and the third is focus.

Let's look at attitude first. Put aside your ego and engage the advice of quality advisors. Understand that you are not an expert in all fields. Seek out expert advice and trusted advisors and implement behaviors that are necessary for your success. Make the tough decisions and execute on those decisions.

If I had to be specific and tell you what we believe is the most important part of attitude that would have the biggest impact on your business, it would have to be goal-setting. Nearly every section of this book, in one way or the other, discusses the importance of proper goal-setting.

Apply the lessons in this book to your own life. Surround yourself with positive people in a positive environment, people who support you and what you are accomplishing; read positive and motivating material; listen to educational tapes and CDs; and associate with people who have a positive, can-do attitude and are willing to share their experience and expertise.

The single most important piece of advice I can give you is: do something! Don't wait for it to be perfect. It will never be perfect. Only action will take you where you want to be. Just get started!

The second step is to build a business plan. Don't over-think the plan. Use it to get focused and provide clarity and direction to your pursuit. This will help you understand your market and how your product (or service) can solve specific problems, and provide clarity for your unique selling proposition.

Use this plan to focus your efforts. Before you take any action, ask yourself "Is this in my business plan, and will it get me closer to my goal?" If the answer is no, then why do it? If it has to be done, move it lower on the priority list.

Your business plan is your roadmap into the future. A good plan will tell you where and how to spend your time and will provide clarity on the types of activities and opportunities that are most important to you. Your business plan is a living document. This plan allows you to recognize and capitalize on opportunities as they become available.

Remember, a great business plan that sits on the shelf is useless. A marginal business plan that is well executed will take you a long way toward your ultimate goal.

Finally, get focused! If you focus on the execution of your business plan, you will be clear on what is important. You will know when it is time to refuse business. You will have the ability to better identity the risks in a given opportunity. You will know when to engage referral partners and when to do it yourself.

Without the plan, one of the biggest problems we face is that of scattering our resources. You can only focus on and do one or two things well at any given point in time. Your plan should clearly identify what those activities are. Be clear on what you want, be focused on what you want and be disciplined in staying on course.

After you address your attitude, create your business plan and focus your efforts, you will find that you have addressed all the other attributes in this book. Spend your time on your attitude, with special attention to goal-setting, create your plan and stay focused. Know what is important and let the other "stuff" take a back seat.

Hundreds of thousands of people like you have already used these principles and experienced dramatic increases in sales volumes, more satisfaction in their dealings with customers and co-workers and greater awareness of their own strengths and weaknesses. They have an increased ability to help people find solutions to their problems and are more adept at identifying new opportunities.

ACCEPT THE CHALLENGE

This first step requires your *personal commitment* to this challenge and *belief* in these principles. Their success is a proven fact, and you can learn to put them to work for you. Of course, any skill takes practice, and you cannot realistically expect to put all of them into effect immediately. However, the minute you start to treat people they way *they* want to be treated, you will start to see immediate results. We encourage you to accept this opportunity to strengthen your business competencies!

MAKE A PLAN

Once you have accepted the challenge, you need a plan to incorporate these techniques into your business. Although we have provided you with an extremely simple, effective method of identifying behavioral styles, it does take some practice. That is why we suggest you begin to incorporate what you have learned about behavioral styles into your business activities.

COMMIT TO GROWTH

"Change is inevitable ... growth is optional." We love that saying because it's true. Right now, you have the option to "finish the book" and get on with the rest of your life and career. After all, this is close to the last paragraph. However, you also have the option to take this moment and make a life-changing decision. You may decide to *keep learning* about yourself, your strengths and weaknesses, your natural tendencies to react to both favorable and unfavorable conditions, how you make decisions, how you come across to other people, etc.

Hopefully, you may decide to use this book as a jumping-off point for a new direction in your career. If that thought excites you, we urge you to visit our site: http://www.yourbusiness-coach.net and learn how to applied these principles in all phases of business, including prospecting, networking, marketing, communications, customer service, referral building, client loyalty, hiring, management, leadership, etc.

May you walk the rest of your journey full of wonder and awe, and may you make many friends along the way.

Here's wishing you continued success!

CONFERENCE STORIES

Allergy and Respiratory Center
HEALTH CARE

Dr. Given credits success of the Allergy and Respiratory Center to the concept of Kaizen, a Japanese term for continuous gradual improvement in work processes, and a visit to Disney World fifteen years ago. "My children enjoyed the rides and the Disney characters. I appreciated how investment, planning and careful execution could result in such a high level of efficiency and professionalism of the entire customer experience." From that point began the practice of weekly office meetings with both business staff and patient care personnel. In an atmosphere of mutual respect, they focus on providing quality patient care and respect, managing each step of the patient experience from the time the patient walks into the office until the time he or she leaves. A sampling of these steps include filling out forms, telephone contacts, payment arrangements, medical interview process, medical education, patient communication techniques, medical record keeping, prescription writing and scheduling appointments. "Through the analysis process, improvements can come in a number of ways – first, a step in the process may be no longer necessary, second, it could be done better, third, it could be done more easily, forth, it could be done by another worker, thus freeing a higher paid or more skilled worker to focus elsewhere or fifth, it could be a process that may lend itself to automation. By continuously reviewing our processes, we find improvements in all these levels," says Given.

Patient care is quite different in his office. The entire office works on a Microsoft Windows NT network and utilizes a computerized medical program to create, store and retrieve patient medical records. Each nurse works from his or her own exam room equipped with PC workstation and printer. "In the field of allergy, there is a need for a lot of discussion between care giver and patient. We know that it is important to spend as much time as needed with each patient and yet, for me to do that by myself with every patient is just impossible." Their response has been to invest in a high level of training for nurses. Equipped with this knowledge, technology and support, the nurses perform much of the interview and education processes. Dr. Given and his Nurse Practitioner are then able to focus on those elements of the evaluation – physical examination, clarification of diagnosis and treatment issues, prescribing of medications and whatever else may require their special skills or knowledge. An approach seems to be working "Everyone seems to win with this approach Patients appreciate the unhurried atmosphere and the emphasis on listening and explaining, nurses enjoy the face to face time with the patient and Joe (Nurse Practitioner) and I enjoy the role of teacher and supervisor" says Given.

"We began working on this in 1996 when there were no electronic medical records! We were flying by the seat of our pants but it was fun! It was very costly but the result has been a program that really fits our needs and our style of practice." Given points out benefits to automation of medical records such as reduced cost of medical transcription, reduced needs for storage of paper charts, reduced errors and improved overall efficiency.

Asked for advice, Dr. Given answers "There is no one rule but some points that have proven helpful to us are to determine what makes your product or service unique or superior. Hire as many smart people as you can afford. Constantly analyze and improve your business or production processes. Share knowledge with employees and encourage them to move up their levels of responsibilities. Look for applicants with a good attitude, natural intelligence and a willingness to learn. When business processes are broken down into well-defined segments, individuals who may not have completed an advanced degree can become excellent employees.

Dr. Given considers himself very fortunate. "I'm happy to have a job I love and people with whom to share it."

Aztek

MARKETING COMMUNICATION – WEB SITE DESIGN

Launched in 1997, Aztek never experienced a decline in business numbers even when others were going out of business. Because of the change in the business climate, however, and because customers were asking Aztek to do things outside the normal aspects of the business, the company realized there was a need to refocus. They analyzed what they were doing right and then moved into the market communications side of the business because "customers pushed them there."

To accomplish this, they hired key individuals – a total of eight added – who could help them move forward into the desired areas, allowing people to focus by reducing multitasking. They developed an account service team to focus on customer related issues, expanded the sales organization, and added personnel to the design team and the I.T. side of the business. They also relocated offices into an environment that better reflected the culture they were trying to create.

Aztek has learned to focus on core competency, but to be all things to all people using strong relationships – all clients are important and need to be treated the same. Aztek points out that having a variety of customers in many industries keeps the ideas fresh. The results have been outstanding in completion rates, dynamic/application based solutions, up time on hosting, quarterly goals exceeded every quarter in 2002, and a revenue growth of 22%-37% in the past three years.

Kevin Latchford, Director of Sales, stresses the importance of strong customer service, "Never close a door on a relationship." All design and development is done by fulltime employees so the customer has many points of contact with all people within the company. All customer questions are answered by the person who is responsible for the issues. Aztek has plans in place to expand their Northeast Ohio presence to Baltimore and Cincinnati over the next six months.

Bonnie Cohen Ceramic Design

CERAMIC TILE & CREATIVE DESIGN FOR ENDOWMENT & FUND RAISING

B onnie Cohen is a designer and fine artist who creates decorative ceramic sculptures and handmade tiles that are sold in galleries and museums. Even though her work was featured in several national publications and sold well in galleries, Cohen wanted to expand her business to include large commercial installations and corporate commissions.

Technology provided the key element to expanding by opening up a whole new market for her designs. It started with the development of her website. Linking to and from several other larger websites, Cohen's site generated national inquiries about her work and within one year; she had obtained four large commissions to design donor recognition and fundraising walls. She uses e-mail, digital photography and conference calling to create and revise design details for these projects. For example, Cohen is currently working on a commission for the Jewish Seniors Agency of Rhode Island with the architect in Washington, D.C., the interior designer in New Hampshire and the signage company (doing the installation) in Maine. In Cohen's words, "Five years ago, I would never have dreamed of working on a project of this caliber from my studio in Akron, Ohio." Even though she may be hundreds of miles away, she can allow the client to "virtually" visit her studio every day to see how their project is coming along, ensuring the personal touch and passion she brings to the work.

Cohen has learned that it is important to balance your personal goals and others expectations. Her advice to other businesspersons includes: don't be afraid to hire the best help. Stick to what you do best and what you are passionate about, don't be afraid to spend money to make your image more professional, and don't let criticism get you down.

Bright.Net
INNOVATION AND REACHING OUT

It's not unusual in the software business to discover the product you need doesn't exist—and then write it yourself anyway. John Clarke, General Manager, found of Bright.net, made the most of it when his creative challenge came along.

Since taking care of 20,000 Internet Service Provider customers is no small responsibility, Alex and his team realized they needed serious protection against hacking and attacking. Being unable to locate anything that fit their unique needs as an ISP, they created one and called i-Trap. Turned out they weren't the only ISPs in the country who needed that kind of security.

But it wasn't just protection the i-Trap solution offered. The methodology Alex and his team created offers automated functionality that saves staff from having to monitor reports and screen out false alarms. It lets users access network traffic logs so they know where to start looking for intrusions. And with the highly detailed reports available, areas of the network that had never before been accessible were open to scrutiny, so improvements in performance became possible. For the first time, ISPs could afford to outsource intrusion protection without giving up control.

Not content to sell locally, Bright.net folks decided to "get more feet on the street" by creating a completely new DBA for the dealer channel that's now taking them into the national market.

Advice to entrepreneurs: Focus on the function! Let the technology worry about itself as you focus on the needs of the customers—and make sure what you build is flexible enough to change with the market.

Brulant

PROFITABILITY

It was a mistake, though not immediately obvious. As soon as Len Pagon realized that the partnership he'd formed was disastrous to the health of his digital strategy and consulting business Brulant, he cut his losses immediately.

After dissolving the partnership, Len and his team set out to re-align costs with expenses. In the face of a sagging economy with no relief in sight, they decided to position the company as a regional leader and pay close attention to sales from existing relationships. First steps included recreating a strong management team (from operations to sales and marketing to finance) and focusing on short-term intense projects that took full advantage of Brulant's trademarked "Time to Value" methodology for delivering fast results.

Revenue streams that used to come largely from industry were now diverted to issue from new sources in the consumer/retail, financial services, healthcare and government sectors. Focusing on these industries allowed them to work with higher-level executives, and they began to grow again slowly. Gradually as revenues solidified, they added programmers, products and practices (including business intelligence and Oracle).

Results: 97% growth over last year. Len's thoughts: The Company is the people. Help build your own leaders. Hit singles and doubles; don't worry about home runs. Think more critically before you make a decision. Doing the small things well gives a company substance.

We've all heard the advice to narrow your niche and grow. Len's take on that: Focus on just one or two things—that gets everyone focused. Then don't waste time, just take action.

Cardinal Commerce

INNOVATION AND REACHING OUT

What have you bought online lately? A lot of people still can't get past their fear of security issues in virtual purchasing—and that includes a lot of the merchants who want to sell you things! That's because up until now, those merchants have had to assume 100% of the responsibility for any credit card losses that occurred because of fraud in online transactions (where the card itself wasn't used).

Michael Keresman III and his co-founders put Cardinal Commerce on the map with the answer to merchants' prayers. They saw the need, did the research and developed a solution that literally takes the risk out e-commerce for merchants.

The product, which is both software and a methodology, permits credit-card-issuing banks and the consumers who use their cards to write an airtight verifiable contract for every transaction made without a card. The authentication process works with today's approaches and is ready for tomorrow's as well—eye scans, thumbprints, voice recognition, and so on—and can be leveraged for multiple applications such as pay-at-the-pump, biometrics systems, mobile phones, and so on.

When Michael accepted the challenge of making Cardinal Commerce the world leader in authentication services, he applied some lessons he'd learned earlier: pull together a Board of highly experienced business leaders who'll brainstorm ideas, help you map your course, and call you on your mistakes—before they kill the dream.

His advice to other entrepreneurs: Build a strong foundation. Don't try to do it alone—get the best advisors. Then listen to them. And make sure to leverage your product to create additional revenue streams from different applications, different markets.

Continental Cuisine

MEDITERRANEAN RESTAURANT

Everyone in the Sebbagh family cooks – the parents and the sons all enjoy the same skills and interest in healthy food. Noticing at their church's yearly cookout how much the church members enjoyed the Mediterranean foods and being in need of a way to support their parents, the sons decided that owning a restaurant would be a good business strategy.

So, in 1998 they opened a deli style restaurant that allowed for a small number of dine-in customers and provided carryout service. As the business grew, Ata Sebbagh and his family, in the words of the Mayor who presented them with the 2000 Mayor's Award for the Outstanding Eatery, "built relationships with customers that almost equal the quality of the food."

In 2002, they leased the space next to them and expanded into a full service restaurant in addition to the carry out service, allowing them to create a customer environment for more formal dining and increasing the number of people served by between 200 and 300%. Roughly, 40% of their business is delivery/take-out and is facilitated by the new/improved point-of-sales equipment system. The sons both graduated from the University of Akron and are experienced IT people, saving $10K-$17K by modifying the software themselves.

They have learned that it was more work than expected – not an 8 a.m. to 5 p.m. job – and that the growth came from word of mouth – not advertising. When asked what he would tell other businesspersons, Ata Sebbagh feels that being disciplined is as important as having knowledge of the business and also being able to look ahead as well as taking a chance. You must have a good product, spend money the right way, and as an employer you have the responsibility for each employee's well being.

DecisionPoint Marketing and Research
MARKET RESEARCH AND CONSULTING SERVICES

During the past few years, DecisionPoint had to react to the economic conditions and reconstruct themselves into a full service research organization. In the past using telephone data and focus groups, the previous company, Data for Decisions in Marketing, Inc. struggled with profitability and growth. In addition, their customers needed strategic insight and were asking for full service – not just data collection services. They decided to refocus and move the business from data gathering to full service: identifying the problem, doing the research and interpreting the data.

During the transition, DecisionPoint created the best video lab in the country and a web usability room that allows organizations to watch and learn how their websites are used. Other products include doing site surveys, along with data mining to evaluate how products are used or to determine other uses for existing products. Lawyers are joining the focus group process for mock jury selections to understand better how juries deliberate. The quality and depth of customer relationships has improved, because clients are changing their business processes in response to the results of their research. DecisionPoint has signed a ten year lease and now considers all of their business relationships as long term – not short term. Cash flow has improved, sales are up 37% from last year and they are now moving into the national market using what they have learned in Northeast Ohio.

Asked what they have learned, Amy Merrill answered, "Treat time as a precious commodity, because it is easy to get involved and let the business suffer. Manage the banks." They found that local community banks were not as supportive of small business as the large regional banks. And what advice would she give? Experienced and secure businesswomen are great mentors. Hire people who are passionate about what they do. Relationships and energy count for everything. Referrals are golden. When things get busy, don't work in the business, work on the business. And always remember, "Your customers are the golden nugget, they typically don't care about what upper management thinks is important- listen to their voice regularly"

Interactive Media Group

INNOVATION

Leaping to conclusions that pay off is a practice Andrew Holland and his team at EYEMG put to work with consummate skill in their web-development business. In the nine years they've been at it, they've redefined "reinvention"—it's now their middle name.

Originally serving customers as a computer hardware service and computer-based training company, the guys at EYEMG gradually noticed more and more businesses catching on to the Internet as a serious marketing tool. Never the follower types, they jumped on the bandwagon ahead of many others and, using creative marketing techniques like a sandwich-boarded sales rep walking the Galleria, soon became a premier provider of web design and development to some of the largest industrial companies in the Ohio valley.

Always value providers—and not the lowest-priced ones—Andrew and his team in the last couple of years started noticing something else. As the Internet love-fest filtered down to the mid-sized business, they saw a whole new market in the middle—but realized that cost would be more of an issue for this level of companies.

In true EYEMG fashion, they engineered another transformation: using low-cost, high-reliability open source tools, they developed a do-it-yourself product called "eyemg.Compose" that lets authorized employees add, delete and edit website content and then publish it themselves, saving dramatic amounts of time over previous methods and affording contributors pride of ownership—which always inspires people to do their best and give more, which in turn means companies tend to keep more of their knowledge capital if an employee leaves.

Imagining—and then creating—win-win situations is what EYEMG is all about. Andrew's observations for others: Watch carefully. Look for trends, listen to your customers and respond quickly. Most of all, care.

United Security Management Services, Inc.
SECURITY GUARDS AND RELATED SUPPORT SOFTWARE

S erving companies' businesses in Northeast Ohio since 1971, the locally owned security guard company United Security Management Services, Inc. realized a need in the marketplace for technology solutions founded on the cornerstone of information and speed. Security incidents and missed guard hours can be costly. "Immediate knowledge is power."

Knowing the importance of instant notification of incidents and deciding to diversify into software solutions that can be sold to other security companies, United Security developed two new products. The Telephone Incident Reporting System (TIRS) provides the solution to transform any phone into a simple to use interface that automates all reporting immediately and implements follow-up response calls to management via phone, fax, pager and e-mail in minutes. The Guard Patrol Information Systems (GPIS) monitors guard tours through automated monitoring devices such as wands and buttons. In the event an exception occurs, such as a missed tour, the system instantly notifies the correct persons via cell phone, pager, PDA and/or e-mail. Clients are now more efficient getting needed information to the correct parties and are able to manage liability and risk. The incident "questions" can be customized for each client. There are a standard eight possible events with eight questions for each event. Used proactively, TIRS also serves as a remedy for preventing repeat incidents.

These new products have resulted in new recurring revenue streams and expanded geographic reach for United Security, along with providing technologically advanced solutions for the entire security industry.

United Security has been surprised with how well TIRS has been received. When asked for advice, Ralph Brislin, EVP, answered, "Don't be under funded. Stay focused!" In hindsight, they would not have launched the two programs at the same time. "GPIS was sold by an enthusiastic person making it difficult to deliver up to expectations."

Unicall International Inc.
INTEGRATED MARKETING

I n April of 1999, Ben Harris established Unicall International, Inc., the direct marketing and call center company, to provide the marketplace with an expert tele-services resource. Typical of most startup companies, Unicall needed financing, methodology, people infrastructure, business development, marketing support and a sales process. Without a "seed" client the challenge to succeed was daunting.

Unicall has made phenomenal use of technology to attract new customers and grow its customer base, including customers outside the local region. Unicall optimized its website to rank high with the major search engines, ran and runs targeted pay-per-click marketing campaigns, and used e-mail blasts to encourage prospect inquiries. They have been able to provide world-class service and compete with larger call centers, because Harris had the foresight to invest in advanced digital call switching technology. Unicall also has established the design subsidiary, Lunar Cow, with complete turnkey marketing solutions for clients, assuring brand consistency and high quality. They have also built proprietary development tools and a ten-step methodology – time-to-deploy is shortened without sacrificing quality. This provides faster return on investment for both the client and Unicall. Now positioned to gear up the Internet sales channel almost at will, Unicall is experiencing consistent revenue and margin increases. They have gained several Fortune clients, word-of-mouth referrals are high and client retention is over 85%. And now, customers have the ability to measure the success of campaigns. Unicall clients realize an industry-defying 10% sales yield on 20% campaign response.

When asked about lessons learned, Harris advises, "Clients value having a complete marketing program and the ability to gauge results. Proactive communication with clients ensures that expectations are exceeded. Getting paid up front minimizes collection effort and cash flow difficulties. Startup managers need a working knowledge of financial metrics and reporting, and especially cash flow management. Develop `business protection' documents early."

TimeWare, Inc.
INNOVATION

It morphed three times before Michael Farhat's software reached the shape that's really putting his company TimeWare on the map. From project management tool to insurance quoting mechanism, the market kept pushing him in different directions. At last his product matured into RMS, a biometric (because it uses thumbprints for IDs) product that helps HR manage labor-intensive workforces.

Michael's main concerns were making the product painless to buy and big on ROI. Because he stayed nimble, when he discovered biometric capability he added it immediately and then worked on shortening implementation time from months to days. And talk about ROI: one health care facility saved 10% on it payroll cost and paid for the software in the first month.

While they were at it, Michael and his team came up with another idea: they're replacing traditional time-punching clocks with a biometric equivalent called BioScreen™ that's priced big and selling like hotcakes. The system combines time clock functions with computer smarts and uses touch-screen and audio technology along with biometric fingerprinting to track employee attendance. Even better, it neatly integrates all the functions of its host computer system, including access to all existing databases. That means, among other things, employees can easily view their personal data (accrued vacation, sick time, etc.) at the same time they clock in.

Michael regrets he didn't realize sooner that labor-intensive industries so needed what he could offer—that he didn't look right away for the most painful problems that needed solving. His advice to others: Work hard and be honest with yourself and with others. Be resilient—it's essential to success. Be willing to change based on what you discover.

RADcom, Inc.

PROFITABILITY

I t's easy to dream, but hard to make it happen. When Bob and Angie Dianetti dreamed up RADcom as a technical writing contracting service, they planned for success and found some, but six years later saw that it wasn't quite what they'd hoped. Never the kind of people to give up, they decided to find out why.

After studying their pricing and profits compared to other companies in the same industry, they realized the advice they'd gotten to change their business model was solid, so they set out to follow it.

Instead of trying to snag every price-dependent deal that came along, they started focusing their sales efforts on existing customers who already saw value in the products and services they were offering. They raised their prices to accommodate a new guideline for marking 50% profit on every deal.

The advice? Get to the sales fundamentals. Identify what is "good business," then pursue it relentlessly. For RADcom that meant focusing on the fundamentals of the sales process 8 hours a day and doing it with measurable repeatable processes.

They made the leap of faith and found that the new approach and raising their prices really was—even in a cash poor market—the answer to profitability. Their latest revenue report shows a 42% growth in sales, 30% growth in profit, and the highest billings in the company's history.

Bob is happy to share the insight they've gained: You must really believe in your product and service and in your ability to deliver it to those who need it. Then work smarter *and* harder. And on a personal note: Don't get emotionally involved in your business: remember it's only a means to an end.

Software Answers
INNOVATION

I t pays to keep your eyes open. Paul Chaffee found that out when he noticed that the State of Ohio's plan to replace the software in its public schools failed to make progress and lost its funding that's when he and his Software Answers team saw their chance. Tapping into their creativity and significant experience in the educational market, they got work and invented a web-enabled software called "ProgressBook." Developed with teacher feedback, its captures the newest state-standards educational practices and is quickly becoming known across Ohio as an excellent tool for teachers.

Designed to serve as a grade book, lesson plan and student information system, and the new K-12 software had to be designed to overcome objections from multiple constituencies in the academic community. After piloting it with the Nordonia and Akron school districts, Software Answers submitted a strategic plan and won first place in the growth division of the Northeast Ohio 2002 Business Challenge.

Working closely with the Ohio Data Acquisition Sites (school-owned providers of computer software, training and support for over 95% of the Ohio public schools), Software Answers eventually won over more than 60% of the sites, and they are now also partnering with the Management Council of the Ohio Education Computer Network (the collective of all 23 DA-Sites) to develop a Special Education addition to ProgressBook.

Even though there was a time they were afraid it was all over—they expected to run out of money with 3 months of work left in the project—they didn't even consider failing on the promises they'd made to Data Acquisition. They knew there was nothing else out there that could provide this level of functionality, so they kept the dream alive. Paul says teamwork—the employee bond—is why they made it.

———

Tell Companies, Ltd.

INNOVATION

Every city has its share of eyesores: structures that once housed giant operations and when abandoned become host to drug traffickers and homeless. The decade-long-empty B. F. Goodrich building took that prize in downtown Akron. Until, that is, Paul Tell Jr. and Paul Tell Sr. decided to take a chance.

A new client of theirs, Advanced Elastomer Systems (AES) was moving to Akron in 1994 and needed a secure home for its high-tech operations. Armed only with a vision and determination, Tell Companies bought the B. F. Goodrich building from the city for $1 and set to work.

First, they secured the partnership of several area banks (First Star, First National, Charter One) on what was deemed a risky investment. Then they gutted all but the framework and supporting pillars and grids, and recreated the building with everything from modern HVAC to security systems and, on the inside, even gave AES glass walls.

Tell Companies signed up their own Kids Play as the second tenant because AES wanted its employees to have on-site child-care. From there, the building took off to its current 90% occupancy. When additional parking was needed, Tell Companies built a sky-bridge to adjoining land.

As part of the visionary project, Tell Companies worked closely with the City of Akron, which invested $4 million in recycling/cleanup initiatives to help with the project and in tax incentive programs to bring more new business to downtown.

The finished building, now known as a "bookend" of a revitalized downtown Akron, was a huge personal and business risk for all concerned. Mistakes? Of course. Issues? Absolutely. Worth it? Unquestionably. Hard?

"If it was easy," says Paul Tell, Sr., "anyone could have done it."

Neighborhood Manufacturing
INNOVATION

Neighborhood Manufacturing as both concept and reality came from loss. Neighborhood was Superior Tool Company's nameless manufacturing facility, located in a low income, residential neighborhood on the near west side of Cleveland.

When imports from Taiwan and China resulted in a severe loss of volume, Superior was forced to re-think Neighborhood's mission. The semi-skilled workforce at Neighborhood was earnestly looking for ways to grow and prosper. They cared. "Invest in us and our community," they said. "Train us...we will make you money. We have skills...use them. We have expertise...use us."

Inspired, the owners decided to market and re-position Neighborhood as a separate strategic business unit for Superior. What makes Neighborhood unique is that it takes advantage of the large supply of inner-city workers interested in flexible scheduled work close to their homes. Most of the employees walk to work. Superior implemented an ongoing program to train and develop the employees with the objective of creating a community environment in the workplace. At Neighborhood, the managers of the facility are employees from the neighborhood…an opportunity for leadership that is typically not readily afforded this group at other jobs.

Neighborhood's innovation is more than just a building full of machinery and people. The Neighborhood model was extended with the introduction of Lean Manufacturing and a complete revision of the Employee Incentive System. Lean has led to a cleaner, trimmer company. While the commitment to velocity existed before Lean's implementation, the program has placed powerful tools in the hands of the workforce to operate "on the edge."

So, pick a compelling business topic: The role of manufacturing in the region; outsourcing; inability of firms to hire and retain; the ability of primary manufacturers to differentiate with added value services; or, unemployment. Neighborhood's model suggests alternatives.

Professional Travel Inc. (PTI)
COMPREHENSIVE TRAVEL MANAGEMENT

As most of us are aware, a combination of events, including Internet sales of airline tickets, the airlines' discontinuation of travel agency commissions, and, finally, the September 11th terror attack all had put increasing pressure on the travel industry.

In order to stay in business and keep their staff, the owners of Professional Travel Inc. (PTI) reviewed their options and decided not to panic and lay off staff. Instead, Mr. Sturm (President & CEO) and his team instituted temporary pay cuts by reducing the hours worked by all employees, making sure that employee benefits would be protected and alternate work arrangements encouraged. Having developed a culture of mutual respect and trust over the years, management knew the value of keeping the lines of communication open with their most important assets – their employees. They were honest about the "new" environment in which they were all working.

Because of financial strength, planning and employee loyalty in difficult times, PTI was able to acquire agencies and some clients of agencies that were going out of business in the harsh travel environment. They consolidated some of the offices as new employees moved into existing offices, along with opening new offices in other locations in greater Cleveland and the state to accommodate the new business.

PTI knows that both the company and employees can benefit when the culture is built on trust and caring. Employees learned how far the company and its management team would go to keep good workers. A testimony to the success of the PTI focus on their people is that the average tenure of the employees is nine years – a long time for people to stay in the industry. "Working at Professional Travel is more like being a member of a family."

NCS DataCom
MANAGED INTEGRATED NETWORK SERVICES PROVIDER

Many service providers offer network management as an "add on" to their focus on providing services such as e-mail, web hosting, and website development. In business since 1987,

NCS DataCom looks into the marketplace and listens to their customers – commercial customers of all sizes – to identify potential needs. They review available technology and either develop or innovatively integrate available services, offering them as individual or bundle service options to their customers.

For example, one recent innovative product release that exemplifies NCS's business approach is the identification and implementation of a secure remote access product (SRA), then adding features to the existing proven technology to provide a unique solution. Unlike most remote access products, this SRA – from Neotris with value added input from NCS – is web based, can be made available to businesses of all sizes at a reasonable cost, does not require firewall construction and is compliant with HIPAA security law. The information security is increased because of the capability of identifying workgroups and discretely defining accessibility for each.

The NCS team has learned that the customer comes first. When you stay close to your customer, it is easier to identify a need in the market and focus your efforts on solving meaningful issues for that customer. Their primary vision has been to provide the best solution for their customer. They stay focused on knowing their market and controlling their growth so that they don't dilute the value they add for their customers.

Andy Lingenfelter from NCS advises other businesspersons to, "Be flexible when evaluating the market and keep the big picture in sight. A couple of different applications, when integrated, result in a service to be provided. Take traditional proven and stable technologies and use them in creative and unique ways."

OnlyOne
MANAGED COMMUNICATION SERVICES

It is a vision of the future of communications that drives Warren Carter, President and co-founder of the cutting-edge joint-venture franchise OnlyOne. The service brings all of your communications into a single number for work, home, fax, cell, pager, voicemail, conference calling, voice messaging and e-mail. OnlyOne allows phone number portability with privacy and complete communications services at cost-effective prices.

In the early 1980s, Carter founded Cleveland-based Voice-Tel and distributed service through 275 local points of presence – franchisees. Through these vested partners – their local sales of local numbers, one-on-one training and local service and support – the network grew and Voice-Tel was sold in 1997. Most of the OnlyOne Management Team partnered with Carter in Voice-Tel and are anxious to surpass their previous successes. They have an appreciation for the local Managing Partners and have structured an unprecedented joint-venture model of franchising where the risks and rewards are fairly shared. The Managing Partner earns additional equity and managements' compensation is based on the success of the local Partner. OnlyOne is different because of the method of deployment, not the product or technology. To date, OnlyOne has partnered in Cleveland, Akron, Columbus, and Cincinnati, Ohio; Atlanta, Georgia; Denver, Colorado; Birmingham, Alabama; and Charlotte, North Carolina.

When asked what he has learned, Carter answers, "The distribution system is the `magic.' Business relationships have become personal relationships making for stronger real partnerships." He was surprised that it was hard to raise money and has found that most partners were landed through referrals, not through web marketing. Carter advises other business persons "Don't ever quit. Build on a solid foundation. Take whatever time is needed to do it right. Plan conservatively. Multiple financial supporters are an advantage over a single capital source. `Partner' decisions are healthier."

5iTech

INNOVATION AND NEW MARKETS

What good is technology if no one knows about it? And there is no one who can effectively bring it to market? When the former Soviet Union disbanded, scientists there kept on working—and often, our former foes develop some really interesting new technologies. Problem was, the best place to market their discoveries was in the U.S., and with culture, language and distance interfering, the likelihood of that happening for any given project was slim to none.

Leon Polott, a Russian immigrant, educated at Oberlin and the University of Texas Law School, was representing large US companies and a group of Russian physicists when he realized the hidden potential of bringing Russian technologies to the US market—and conceived an idea and a company called 5iTech.

In his practice as an attorney in Cleveland, Leon was instrumental in the establishment of Imalux, Inc., an Ohio-based medical imaging company, with technology imported from the Soviet Union. He decided to take what he'd learned about success and apply it in a systematized way to new technologies he'd uncover. His contacts among scientists and in research centers and labs in the former Soviet Union were more than happy to cooperate.

5iTech selects only those technologies that appear to have strong potential in large markets of $500 million-plus. It follows the legal steps to license and transfer the technology to the U.S. where it then finds access to capital and to licensing partners and helps the new U.S. company bring the technology to market.

Recently the company took on a promising biomedical device product that lets doctors test for allergic reactions before they prescribe certain drugs.

Interest in 5iTech's work is high in the government sector, especially through the U.S. State Department's non-proliferation efforts. Leon is very pleased his company can promote healthy business interactions between the two former enemies in a way that also creates jobs and new business opportunities for U.S. citizens.

Lessons? Be in the right place at the right time—pay attention and get to work.

MrExcel.com
MICROSOFT EXCEL KNOWLEDGE AND APPLICATION DEVELOPMENT

If the IT market is down, then how did Mr.Excel.com grow 400%? This is the story of how Mr.Excel.com boomed in a bombed industry.

Bill Jelen was known as the "go to" guy for Excel solutions at Telxon where he worked. With his understanding of the hidden power lying just beneath the Excel desktop, Jelen realized how much time, money and frustration Excel users wasted. He decided to launch MrExcel.com where people could ask Excel questions that he would answer, hopefully generating enough consulting jobs to make as much money as he was in his corporate position.

As the site grew – with Jelen working in shorts and a t-shirt and being there when his kids came home from school – he realized he was still trading time for money. To exponentially increase his revenue while decreasing the amount of time spent programming and charging for the hour, Jelen initiated a plan which included creating and packaging products and services from what he already had (he harvested and indexed over 12,000 questions and answers). He published for a specific segment by creating the ultimate real-world users manual for making sense out of data. He has licensed a simple wizard program for the automotive dealer market that is being used in automobile dealerships.

Jelen stresses that he capitalizes on signature strength by understanding his "crusade" and the emotions his customers go through in using his product/system. He differentiates himself from the competition by knowing who his customers are and building their trust. And he has cloned his system by taking his Excel crusade and building a story and a system around it.

Jelen says, "It's not impossible to see exponential growth. The key lies in sound customer-centered marketing strategy and your expertise and passion for what you do."

Gateway Title
REACHING OUT

You don't always get what you bargained for when you start your own company. Because Rachel Torchia already had some solid relationships with a good number of real estate agents, she figured she could count on their business when she struck out on her own to found Gateway Title Company.

Fate had other plans.

Getting business from existing relationships was to remain a pipedream. What Rachel hadn't counted on was that the agents she knew so well were doing business with her former company for a reason: they liked getting paid for each referral they made—to the tune of numbers that Rachel knew a startup couldn't match—and might never be able to.

Undaunted, Rachel looked into her crystal ball—and did a lot of legwork—to find another approach. Now's the time, she thought. Time to re-think. Time to get going. When she finally found her answer, she rewrote her business plan to reflect what she'd discovered: a whole new market that wasn't being served.

Turned out most title companies had no interest in working with owners selling their own homes (FSBO – for sale by owner) because they couldn't count on the real estate agents sending them business. In three years, she developed an FSBO title kit, produced marketing collateral, and slowly gained a foothold in the market. She even refinanced to keep the business going.

But she realized she needed something more and couldn't simply wait for things to happen, so she called the Plain Dealer whose readers included her perfect market: owners who want to sell their own houses. It was just the jumpstart her business needed. Rachel is now very proud that she took the bull by the horns and was able to pay back her investors within two years. The lesson: change directions when you hit the wall!

Physicians Medical Service Bureau, Inc.
REACHING OUT

They had a big problem: balancing revenues against growing costs. Physicians Medical Service Bureau (PMSB) had to keep adding more people and more space with every increase in billings. The scales were tipping too far, and after 20 years of steady growth, critical mass had been reached. They knew it was time to do something. Jay Chambers came up with a brilliant solution to his company's problem: let's change the way we do business.

The new approach is based on having customers enter their own data into a web-hosted version of PMSB's software. They had Software Answers create a Virtual Private Network (VPN) so that clients could access systems securely through the web, thus eliminating potential backups with phone lines and keeping clients in strict compliance with HIPAA privacy requirements.

All of that was great news. In fact, because they were able to reduce operating costs so much, the project had a payback time of only 60 days. Even though at first revenues went down slightly, profits went up. But the real kicker was that with the new functionality PMSB had opened up a whole new world of prospects—they could now serve customers nationwide.

PMSB knew that customers always have options. So they made sure all of theirs were allowed to choose whether to participate in the new functionality or keep it the old way. It was critical to put customer desires first, even if it meant letting them walk away.

Jay says tells entrepreneurs to believe in what you're doing. "That makes it fun." And remember, he says, it's okay to charge higher rates and turn down some business. Looking back at what PMSB has just accomplished, he says: "It's good to know that I can decide how much money I want to earn."

———

Foundation Software
PROFITABILITY

In the construction industry, as in most, accounting software is one of the first things you buy. Fred J. Ode knew there was nothing more critical than controlling costs and monitoring cash flow in labor-intensive industries, because he'd been helping construction companies with their accounting for years. It seemed natural at some point to write his own financial software—Foundation Software—and sell it to them.

But the selling wasn't as easy as he'd thought. The first job he got was an hourly-rate gig for a steel contractor for the World Trade Center in 1985. Customers of his former employer's software supported him and his first associates for a long time—85% of their revenue came from custom programming. But Fred just wasn't sure who else would buy their product or services.

Three years and hundreds of phone calls later, he got his first product sale to a construction customer and got a real start—on the road to the company's current mix of 85% product and 15% services, a much more desirable situation.

In his quest to grow, Fred knew he had to evolve the product—and at some point, bite the bullet and re-write his DOS-based software. He did so in 1990, using SQL Server and adding desirable new functionality. But he knew that no matter how good a product might be, it was always a question of getting it sold.

One of Fred's secrets is to carefully nurture the sales process with a unique approach: he uses an internal sales staff, but because different qualities are valuable in each of the stages of selling—generate/qualify/close—Fred actually uses different people for each stage. He's been so successful—now up to 1500 clients in his totally self-funded business—that 35% of revenue is now new business.

Fred's advice to entrepreneurs: Be the best at one thing. Put people first—have your hiring, education and termination processes firmly in place. And last but not least: Manage by the numbers and watch cash flow.

What else from an accounting guy?...

OEConnection

AUTOMOTIVE OEM PARTS ORDERING PROCESS AND SOFTWARE

Even though the sale of original equipment (OE) auto parts, along with service and repair, provide a huge business for many auto dealerships, the process of ordering, buying and/or selling OE parts among dealers has been inefficient and time consuming due to the human intervention required. OEConnection with its founding partners, DaimlerChrysler, Ford, General Motors, and ProQuest Company has solved this critical business issue for its customers.

Through a single-source Internet portal and powerful transaction software, OEConnection devised a faster and more efficient way for wholesale buyers to order genuine OE parts and for auto dealers to locate and sell parts. The improvement project took hold on the 7th of December 2000, with the founding of OEConnection. CollisionLink®, a web-based service enabling collision shops to transmit orders for OE parts, was launched in May 2001 to serve the wholesale collision repair buyers. By December 2001, the D2DLink® parts locator and procurement product was piloted and four dealers were activated by February 2002. Initially sold through Ford's corporate program, 4,500 Ford dealers were soon on board accessing an inventory database updated nightly and searching 30,000 times each day. GM adopted D2DLink in mid-2002. In 12 months, over 5,000 GM dealer customers were added to the D2DLink program. Within 22 months of existence, OEConnection became profitable, continues to be profitable for straight nine months and OEConnection is positioned to offer more supply chain products to the automotive industry.

When asked for a list of lessons learned, Chuck Rotuno, CEO, answered, "Deliver products that solve real problems, not hype. Get the right people on the team. Hire professionals, vs. the fashionable." He was surprised by how difficult it is to change behavior, especially with the collision shop personnel. Rotuno also advises, "You can't try to solve too much too soon. Concepts need to be proven to solve real problems. Control the growth. Never underestimate the value and need for hiring and retaining the best employees. Continuous improvement is essential, especially based on customer feedback. Manage by the numbers!"

Fortney & Weygandt, Inc.
GENERAL CONTRACTING (CONSTRUCTION)

Paperwork was a problem. Construction superintendents were inconsistent. It was hand written, not professional and the time-to-office was extremely slow. Dealing with the Project Superintendents who are not typically computer literate, they needed an easy to use system. Bob Fortney, President, and the management team realized that getting better at each and every phase of corporate operations is key to success. If they were more efficient and more productive, the company would be more profitable.

Fortney hired an outside contractor to set up Version 1of the custom-written SuperView program to process project-specific paperwork. Version 2 was completed by inside programmers. The superintendents are on site daily with the other trades people and sync updated information from the field with a two-week look-ahead schedule maintained. Supervisors now claim they can't live without the system. Information, including photos, is now available daily to all parties needing it. Efficiency has greatly improved and clients can access the information as desired. Superintendents can work offline and update at the end of the day; the synchronization is automated and simple. The surprising part is that Version 1 took hours to synchronize daily, while Version 2 takes just minutes.

Fortney, as the company leader and visionary, has learned that he can't get too close to the details in programming the solution. He advises sticking to the functional specifications and not allowing the programming techies to change anything. Make it user friendly so that it will be used.

Fortney also feels that tangible results = tangible rewards. The way to succeed is continuous improvement; nothing is sacred. Surround yourself with good people and employ a team concept. It is working for F& W. They have won the Silver Hammer Award from *Constuctech Magazine* and the Ernst & Young Entrepreneur of the Year Award.

ICBS, Inc.
WEB HOSTING, DEVELOPMENT, AND INTERNET HEALTHCARE

Dr. Jacob Mathew, founder of ICBS, Inc., has found the perfect opportunity to give something back to the community and make a difference in people's lives. Having incorrect data about alternate forms of medical therapy can be life threatening. So, when Mathew's wife, a medical doctor, expressed concern that many patients were referring to Internet for health information and may be receiving incomplete or incorrect information from the web, often biased to promote individual agendas, Mathew decided to develop a website that provides comprehensive information about all aspects of health (combining traditional western medicine with alternative medicine) including drug interaction concerns when combining herbal remedies, alternative and mind-body therapies and holistic living with modern medicine.

The website, http://www.holisticonline.com (with firstholistic.com and epreferredproviders.com) is now used extensively by general public as well as doctors, nurses, patients and others associated with alternative forms of treatment. The website serves as an in-depth introduction to all forms of medicine including many forms of alternative medicine, and treatment information. It is one of the largest free resource databases of its kind in the world. Mathew is being assisted in this venture by a highly trained team of doctors, nurses, yoga practitioners, herbal specialists, stress management experts, etc. who provide unpaid consulting to ensure the accuracy of the data. Mathew has a library of over 1000 books on the subject so he can use material to validate and plan for new features on the website which has grown to over 50,000 pages of content. It receives over 4 million hits/month from over 170 countries, and has received critical acclamation from all over the world.

Mathew says he has "followed his dream" and wouldn't take money from any sponsors for fear that it might cause concern for the objectivity and independence of the site. With a zero dollar-marketing budget, he promoted the site using search engines and a tremendous effort in networking, personal pro-motion, and other strategies to push it ahead of sites that have marketing budget reaching into nine digits. His advice to others includes: have passion for what you do, be persistent, believe in what you are doing, be the best at what you are doing and don't copy someone's idea, and don't listen to the people who say it can't be done.

Lazorpoint, Inc.

NETWORK ENGINEERING SERVICES

After being in business for three years, Dave Lazor felt like he was still a one-man operation. He couldn't seem to find the right people. Business growth was stalled – one step forward and two steps back.

Don Steiner was referred to Lazor as a prospective employee and after getting to know one another, they realized they had a shared vision and cultural values. They made one less than suc-cessful hire before their streak of good hires. They evaluated what was good in those hires, analyzed, formulated and repeated. They initiated personnel profile testing, identified and codified the company culture and values, and initiated and implemented a branding program. They realized that they needed to build the company, not just billable hours. Clients had always liked the results, but Lazor was approaching burnout by doing so much himself.

Clients are now comfortable with Lazorpoint, Inc., not just Dave Lazor, who is no longer the most important guy to the clients. He is now focused on working ON the business, not IN the business. Clients trust the company – that is made up of great people. Since 2000, the business has grown considerably by every measure: from three to ten employees, tripled the office space with new, higher grade quarters, a full-time office administrator and 100% retention.

Lazor learned that success breeds success. Good personnel hires led to additional good hires. The right people "on the bus" make all the difference. He shares that he should have done the right things sooner – gained a clear understanding of the company values and defined the culture as soon as possible. Lazor also suggests making investments wisely – don't fear spending according to a plan. Know and measure the numbers. Measure and consider risk and reward. Build confidence in your clients, your people, your business partners and yourself.

Mustard Seed Market & Café
FULL SERVICE HEALTH FOOD STORE

From a home-based vegetarian catering business started in 1978 with $60 and a cooking pot, husband and wife team, Margaret and Philip Nabors, have grown the Mustard Seed Market & Cafe into the largest retailer of natural and organic products in Northeast Ohio.

In 1981, the Nabors opened a small health food store in Akron's Merriman Valley and named it Mustard Seed Market, drawing from the biblical metaphor that faith is like the tiny mustard seed from which a great tree grows. And the Market grew. In 1989, they relocated the store to an area that was more accessible, had 9K square feet and housed a 60-seat restaurant. Business boomed and in September of 1996, the Nabors made the decision to expand into two stores that became available, adding an additional 22.5K square feet. Upholding the commitment to helping individuals enjoy healthier lives through healthier eating habits, the Market continues to offer an extensive list of cooking classes, lectures and food demonstrations. The success of this store led to another expansion in October 1999 with the opening of the additional Mustard Seed Market & Café in Solon.

From the beginning, the Market's appeal has been trust – consumers can trust the quality of the food and products they buy. The Nabors spend time on the floor with their customers, know what they want and provide one place where all health food and related products can be purchased.

Their advice includes: putting a process in place that ensures that everyone is treated the same (especially important during growth), visit peers to learn from their success and failures, and hire good people who enjoy their work and then let them do it. It is important to have a higher vision and purpose. Their motto is "together, we'll save the world one bite at a time."

COMPANY CONTACT INFORMATION

5iTech
Leon Polott
1768 E. 25th St.
Cleveland
OH 44114

Allergy & Respiratory Center
Dr. John Given
45fourteen Fulton Drive NW
Canton, OH 44718

Aztek
Kevin Latchford
Director of Sales
26040 Detroit Road
Suite 1
Westlake, OH 44145

Bonnie Cohen Ceramic Design
Bonnie Cohen
718 Pine Point Dr.
Akron, OH 44333

Bright.net Internet Providers
Alex Desberg
37 E. Marion Street
Doylestown, OH 44230

Brulant
Len Pagon
President
5595 Transportation Blvd.
Suite 230
Cleveland, OH 44125

CardinalCommerce
Christopher Brown
Director of Finance
6119 Heisley Road
Mentor, OH 44060

DecisionPoint
Amy Merrill
President
3634 W. Market St.
Suite 104
Fairlawn, OH 44333

Continental Cuisine Eatery
Ata Sebbagh
55 Ghent Road
Akron, OH 44333

Fortney & Weygandt, Inc.
Chris Lutjen
31269 Bradley Road
N. Olmsted, OH 44070

Foundation Software
Tracie Kuczkowski
Marketing Director
150 Pearl Road
Brunswick, OH 44212

Gateway Title Agency
Rachel Torchia
8748 Brecksville Rd. #100
Brecksville, OH 44141

ICBS, Inc.
Jacob Mathew
President
24 Canton Road
Akron, OH 44312

Interactive Media Group
Andrew Holland
President
190 N. Union St.
Suite 300
Akron, OH 44304

Lazorpoint, Inc.
David M. Lazor
President
fourteen600 Detroit Ave.
Suite fourteen50
Lakewood, OH 44107

MrExcel.com
Bill Jelen
President
13386 Judy Ave. NW
Uniontown, OH 44685

Mustard Seed Market
Phillip & Margaret Nabors
Owners
3885 West Market Street
Akron, OH 44333

NCS DataCom, Inc.
Andrew Lingenfelter
26391 Curtis Wright Pkwy
Richmond Hts., OH 44143

Neighborhood Manufacturing,
Div. Of Superior Tool Co.
Howard M. Garfinkel
3243 West 33rd St.
Cleveland, OH 44109

OEConnection
Charles Rotuno
President
4150 Highlander Pkwy
Richfield, OH 44286

OnlyOne
Pam Conaway
5755 Granger Rd
Suite 630
Cleveland, OH 44131

Physicians Medical Service
Bureau, Inc.
Jay Chambers
President
6189 Mayfield Road
Mayfield, OH 44124

RADcom
Bob Dianetti
President
1696 Georgetown Road
Unit A
Hudson OH, 44236

Software Answers, Inc.
Paul Chaffee
President
202 Montrose West Ave.
Suite 290
Akron, OH 44321

TimeWare Inc.
Michael Farhat
President
9329 Ravenna Rd.
Suite 4
Twinsburg, OH 44087

Unicall International Inc.
Benjamin C. Harris
President
3250 West Market Street
Suite 205
Fairlawn, OH 44333

United Security Management
Services, Inc.
Ralph F. Brislin
Executive V.P.
fourteen40 Snow Road
Cleveland, OH 44134

ABOUT THE AUTHOR

Ronald Finklestein

AKRIS LLC

http://www.akris.net

Ron Finklestein is President of AKRIS LLC, a company that provides business and technology coaching and consulting using a methodology he developed called 12 Action Steps to Predictable Business Growth. This approach is documented in his book Celebrating Success! Fourteen Ways to a Successful Company.

For over 20 years Finklestein executed consulting services for Fortune 2000 companies. His experience includes projects in the banking, manufacturing, insurance, information technology, healthcare, and government and finance verticals.

In 2001, Finklestein stated AKRIS LLC with the sole focus of bring large company experience, discipline and focus to smaller organization to help them grow and success. His customers call him the Small Business Success Expert.

Today, Finklestein (and his firm) works with clients who desire to systematize and implement predictability in the entire corporate structure: operations, sales, marketing, customer service, and back office processes.

Ron serves as an entrepreneur, author, speaker, trainer and consultant. He may be reached by calling 330-990-0788 or via email: info@yourbusinesscoach.net

CONTRIBUTING AUTHORS

Charles M. Gilmore

PRINCIPAL, AVANTT CONSULTING

Before joining Avantt, Chas accumulated over 35 years of high-technology management experience in US, European and Asian consumer, industrial, software and aerospace markets.

He worked for multinationals such as Schlumberger, Zenith Electronics and Groupe Bull; for mid-sized public and privately held companies such as Heath Company (Heathkit), Alltrista Corporation and YXLON International, and for start-ups.

For the last twenty years, Chas has held senior posts such as COO, CEO and President. His specialty is strategic planning and product development, and he has proven success with strategic realignments. Chas led the successful turnaround and restructuring of a number of firms, as well as overseeing the acquisition and divestiture of product groups and companies.

Known as an out-of-the box thinker, Chas brought change to the organizations he led through unique and highly successful management structures, business models, and new product-line and product concepts. He also guided the redirection of companies, moving them from decaying late-stage companies in stagnant markets to rapidly growing, profitable second-stage companies in new expanding markets—while still preserving and capitalizing on the brand name recognition, infrastructure and human resources of the original company.

Chas has been involved with a number of not-for-profit organizations both as a member of volunteer executive boards and as a consultant. He served on the board of directors for a regional healthcare organization with three hospitals, two nursing homes, two pharmacies and a durable medical equipment supplier. He also was a board member, executive board member and consultant with a regional economic development organization.

As an agent of change, he redefined roles for many team members, thus allowing them to significantly increase their contributions to the organization. Among his accomplishments, Chas counts over a dozen former employees who are now Presidents/CEOs of their own companies.

Chas holds a BS in Physics from Hobart College and pursued advanced business studies at the Harvard Business School and Wharton. He is also the author of numerous texts on electronics technology (McGraw-Hill), served on the boards of directors for a number of organizations, and is the holder of patents related to electronic instrumentation.

cgilmore@avanttconsulting.com, 330-867-9860

Ivana Taylor

THIRDFORCE MARKETING

I vana Taylor has built a business around making pricing and competitive pressures disappear. She has spent the last 17 years re-positioning public, private and equity-funded industrial organizations into new, more profitable markets. She loves the challenge and reward of turning a mature organization in a mature market into a bustling, impassioned competitive force. And so do her clients. Her approach to marketing is grounded in sound strategic principles – but look out for her unorthodox approach to application and implementation.

In 1999, Ivana formed Third Force, a strategic marketing firm that provides its business-to-business clients with a unique and profitable market position that makes them the obvious choice for their ideal customers.

Ivana calls herself an instinctive and intuitive strategist. She sees those subtle decision-points that typically make the difference in who your ideal client will choose; you, your competitor or nothing at all.

Ivana's vision is to make her clients the only game in town.

Ivana holds a Masters Degree in Management from Antioch University, a Certificate in German Language Studies from the University of Munich and a B.S. in Marketing from Pennsylvania State University.

Ivana is an active member of the Akron and Cleveland business communities. She is a member of TEC, Women's Network and National Association for Women Executives. She is also a motivational speaker on team development, leadership and strategic planning.

Ivana Taylor, ThirdForce Marketing
330-472-0981
ivana@thirdforce.net

The Bothwell Group

JOHN M. BOTHWELL PH.D.
PRESIDENT

John M. Bothwell, Ph.D. is an international business trainer, author, and consultant with over 30 years of national and international sales expertise. Dr. Bothwell has combined psychology with his many years of real world selling and sales consulting experience to help business leaders achieve their goals. Dr. Bothwell is an adjunct professor on the staff of Cleveland State University.

As an aggressive problem solver and recognized industry leader, John Bothwell applies his diverse experience and talents to growing his sales-and management-consulting firm. John leads his team in implementing strategies and tactics that achieve both company and individual growth for their clients. Working with a variety of companies from Fortune 500 to start-ups, he has developed insights and skills proven to be successful in real-world settings.

John M. Bothwell, Ph.D. has ISO certification in sales and marketing and is a certified senior manufacturing engineer with the Society of Manufacturing Engineers. Other International accreditations include Certified in Marketing and Sales (CMS), Certified Professional Behavior Analyst (CPBA), Certified Professional Values Analyst (CPVA) and Certified Attribute Index Analyst (CAIA).

By John M. Bothwell Ph.D.
The Bothwell Group, Inc.
440-356-8774
jmb@bothwellgroup.com

Josephine Gilmore
PARTNER/MARKETING CONSULTANT, GROUP GILMORE

Group Gilmore is a private consultancy specializing in strategic marketing for technology products and services. We have over 40 combined years of international experience with technology, from consumer electronics to capital equipment, and we know what it takes to create a sustainable advantage in today's global marketplace. Our services include New Markets & Products, Competitive Intelligence, and Strategic Marketing.

Josephine Gilmore is a multi-lingual marketing strategist with 15 years of international high-tech experience, including e-commerce, telecom, semiconductors and electronics. Her specialties are strategic marketing and market analysis. In addition to her professional work in Europe, Asia and the US, she has also taught professional and university courses in ecommerce and marketing.

Ms. Gilmore holds an MBA in Marketing from Suffolk University and a Master's of International Management from Thunderbird, the American Graduate School of International Management. She is fluent in French, and conversant in Spanish and German.

Josephine.Gilmore@GroupGilmore.com, 330-867-1211

CONFERENCE STORIES AUTHORS

Chris King

PRESIDENT/OWNER, CREATIVE KEYS

A human development specialist, artist, web site developer and designer, storyteller, trainer, consultant, TV announcer, model, mathematician, marketing manager, newspaper editor, salesperson, waitress, writer, speaker and mother of five are some of the personas that have given **Chris King** her creative expertise and lots of material for her presentations.

Chris, who has a Bachelor of Arts Degree in Mathematics from Goucher College and all course work toward a Master of Fine Arts Degree in Studio Art from Kent State University, shares that her true passions are storytelling and the Internet.

Chris has appeared in TV commercials; won art awards at the Cleveland, Massillon and Columbus Museums of Art; was named District 10 Toastmaster of the Year - 1990-91, by Toastmasters International and received the 1997-98 Chapter Member of the Year Award from the Ohio Speakers Forum (a Chapter of the National Speakers Association).

She is a member and the Ohio State Liaison of the National Storytelling Network, past president, current membership chair and webmaster for the Ohio Order for the Preservation of Storytelling (O.O.P.S!), immediate past president of the Greater Cleveland PC Users Group, and is a Certified Group Fitness Instructor with the American Council on Exercise.

If you want more information on Chris' business and/or websites visit:

www.creativekeys.biz (business site)
www.creativekeys.net (information site)
chris@creativekeys.net
(216) 991-8428

Barbara Payne

A friend once pressed her mercilessly to come up with exactly what she planned to tell the people at a Fortune 500 corporation about what she *really* does for companies. He kept pressing her, when suddenly she looked heavenward and it came to her. "I help them find their true voice," she said. "...help them express their true meaning in powerful words."

Thus was born the trademarked tagline Barbara now uses on her corporate website and her marketing materials: "Find your True Voice...and grow your business"™

The ability to write, Barbara says, is a gift. What you do with it depends on who you are. She says hers comes with years of experience learning from smart businesspeople how best to answer WIIFM (what's in it for me?) for her clients' target audiences.

In recognition of her 20 years of accomplishments, Barbara was invited to co-author a book with business gurus Brian Tracy,

Mark Victor Hansen and others. The book is called "Create the Business Breakthrough You Want: Secrets and Strategies from The World's Greatest Mentors," and it's endorsed by well-known business giants like Ken Blanchard (One-Minute Manager) and Dr. Stephen Covey (The 7 Habits of Highly Effective People). It's on the presses right now; you can get your copy in September. You can reach her at Barbara@reallygoodfreelancewriter.com

Barbara Payne, Managing Principal
a ReallyGoodFreelanceWriter.com -
www.ReallyGoodFreelanceWriter.com
Marketing Tips Blog: www.reallygoodfreelancewriter.com/GetMoreCustomers/

Business Blog: www.BlogforBusiness.com
Bioscience: www.BioMedNews.org
Cleveland 440.646.0041
Chicago voice mail/fax 312.416.7965

CONCLUSION

This book was written to give individuals and owners of a small business a road map to improve their personal and corporate performance.

This book consolidates years of business and technology experience from a variety of experts to provide a roadmap for success. This roadmap was created by studying what other companies did to be successful.

Apply these principles and you to can achieve success, add balance in your life, create successful company and prosper while creating the life you want.

BONUS

To receive your free gift valued at $149, go to http://www.yourbusinesscoach.net/course-download.html and fill in the registration information. You will be redirected to a download page. This download is a self-paced course on creating the life you want by implementing the seven attitudes and behaviors of successful people.

www.ingramcontent.com/pod-product-compliance
Lightning Source LLC
Chambersburg PA
CBHW071421170526
45165CB00001B/354